I could have been a stoker for a vertical wimple crimper: Classic tales from Canada

by

Geoff Hill

THUNDERCHILD PUBLISHING
Huntsville, Alabama

I could have been a stoker for a vertical wimple crimper: Classic tales from Canada

Copyright © 2020 by Geoff Hill

Edited by Liana Thompson

ISBN: 9798655715431

Published by Thunderchild Publishing. Find us at https://ourworlds.net/thunderchild_cms/

Cover design by Dan Thompson. Beaver image ID 33097340 © Christopher Doehling | Dreamstime.com

Endorsements

Geoff Hill, Winner of a Labatt's UK travel writing award and a Canada Award: what the critics say

Geoff Hill has an outstanding writing talent with a wicked sense of fun. Brilliant writing, genuinely and originally funny, and a supremely entertaining read.

Martyn Lewis, broadcaster

He has wonderful views on life, a great turn of phrase and a great sense of humour. His off-beat observations and zany outlook on life are laugh-out-loud funny.

John Mullin, *The Independent*

Hill has a voice all his own — both lyrical and lunatic — which casts the world in a new light.

Mark Sanderson, *Independent on Sunday*

Hilarious.

Lois Rathbone, *The Times*

Geoff Hill is a comic genius. I laughed until I cried, my nose bled and I lost control of my bowels. I may well have to kill him when I meet him.

Patrick Taylor, author of New York Times best seller
An Irish Country Doctor

Brilliant. At times laugh-out-loud funny, and at others intensely moving, which is part of Geoff's genius. He's a writer for whom the words highly and recommended were invented.

Brian Page, Mensa magazine

A brilliant read.

Dave Myers, BBC's Hairy Biker

Once upon a time...

On a cold grey morning in the winter of 1992, I was leafing through the News Letter, the daily newspaper of which I was features and travel editor, when I noticed a tiny story at the bottom of page five saying that the International Fund for Ireland was sending a bunch of journalists from Ireland to Canada for three months.

There was a contact number at the bottom for the Irish organiser, so I picked up the phone and called her.

"Here, are there any places left on that scheme?" I said.

"Just one, but we'd need to know by the end of today," she said.

I hung up, and walked into the office of Geoff Martin, the editor.

"Here, boss, how would you feel about me buggering off to Canada for three months? You'd get a great daily series out of it," I said.

"Er, OK," he said, which was typically generous of him. One of the finest editors I've worked for, he had the vision to know that life didn't end at the garden gate.

So off I went, first at the welcoming and brilliant London Free Press in Ontario, then by train and bus first to the west coast and north to the Yukon and Alaska.

I wrote and faxed a story every single day; and when I got home, found most of them crumpled at the bottom of a drawer in the deputy editor's desk.

"No space," he muttered by way of explanation.

After sobbing gently in the corner for a bit, I did get some of them published, they won two UK travel writing awards, and the year after, I went back and travelled east as far as Newfoundland.

This is the first time those stories have been gathered together in one volume. I hope you enjoy them as much as I enjoyed Canada.

Geoff Hill
July 2019

Part One

Ontario

One

It wasn't long before my first taste of what the Canadians call multiculturalism.

Before our Air Canada 747 to Toronto had even moved at Heathrow, Captain Bob Fox was on the intercom, apologising in English for the delay.

Like all airline pilots, Captain Bob had the sort of voice guaranteed to reassure you that everything was all right even if the plane was vertical and stewardesses were whistling past our ears.

Seconds later, chief steward Helen Schriver repeated Bob's apology in French. With a Swedish accent. Then German.

After that, I was expecting instructions on how to put on a lifejacket in Romanian and a Serbo-Croat preview of the in-flight movie, The Rocketeer.

Since there was a splendidly exotic African chap sitting in seat 36B, presumably the movie would be available in Swahili with Urdu subtitles.

In fact it turned out to be appalling in any language. If you ever get a chance, don't go to see it.

It was so bad that I listened to it in French on my headphones, but when that didn't work, I tried the other nine channels until I got to The Barber of Seville, then ordered a pillow, a blanket, and hot towels by the gallon, and had a whisky for breakfast.

By the time I'd turned my watch back five hours to Toronto time and started reading Paul Thoreaux's The Great Railway Bazaar, I felt quite hopelessly gaga. There's a lot to be said for having whisky for breakfast five miles above the Atlantic while listening to Rossini and reading about Iran. And I hadn't even started speaking to the two people on either side of me. He was plugged into Big Country on his headphones, and she was reading Ian McEwan's The Innocent in paperback.

It was easy to imagine histories for them. He was in his mid-thirties, and where his wedding ring should have been, there was a faint band of white skin.

A Scottish engineer, he'd married a secretary from Luton. Five years later they went on a second honeymoon to Athens, where he accused her of flirting with a barman who looked like a slightly used Greek god.

In the tumult of recriminations which followed, she confessed to a fling with her bank manager, a married man in his fifties, a year after her marriage to the engineer.

At the engineer's request, the firm had transferred him to Canada, and now he sat beside me on his way out, sadly nervous at the thought of flinging bridges over frozen gorges in the Northwest Territories.

At home, his wife was watching Eastenders and waiting for the phone to ring.

And the petite blonde woman on my right? She was the wife of the bank manager, of course, fleeing her husband after a spate of mystery phone calls and a hotel receipt found in a jacket pocket.

I should have introduced them, but my attention was distracted by page 88 of The Great Railway Bazaar, in which Thoreaux described a visit to the Kabul Insane Asylum to gain the release of a Canadian who had been put in there by mistake.

"He said he didn't mind staying there as long as he had a supply of chocolate bars; it was better than going back to Canada," wrote Thoreaux.

But it was too late. I was on my way, and there was no stopping now.

Two

Walking out into the Canadian cold for the first time is the antithesis of stepping into a sauna. First you get the breathless wash of cold, then the inside of your nostrils collapsing.

I clutched my traumatised nose in both hands and stumbled to the taxi rank, where I found an ocean liner with wheels driven by a splendidly moustachioed Lebanese man called Simon.

"Nnn Kning Ednard Notel," I said.

"Certainly, sir," said Simon, with some aplomb.

Since the hotel was only about five miles away, I didn't actually need to get into the taxi. I just put my luggage in the boot, walked around to the front of the bonnet, and there I was.

"How big is the engine in this thing?" I asked Simon as I handed him the contents of my wallet.

"Not so big. About five litres," he said.

I checked into my room at the King Edward, had a Molson Export in the bar, and went out for a burger at a place called The Keg with Bill Jermyn, an Irish marketing consultant who'd moved to Toronto when the fleshpots of Cork had somehow palled on him.

By the time we got there my moustache had taken on the consistency of Shredded Wheat which had been left in the freezer, and the only way I could be sure I still had ears was to look in a mirror when we got there.

"Canadians are very informal about going out," said Bill after we'd bought a drink and sat down.

Behind him, a man in a dark three-piece suit jerked nervously across the dance floor, encouraged by his girlfriend's forgiving smile, while on the giant TV above their heads, enormous black men with shaved heads competed to win the national slam dunk contest.

It was difficult to see which was the most pointless exercise, and Bill and I avoided the issue, walking another ear-numbing distance to a nearby Irish bar incongruously called New Windsor House, where owner Jimmy McVeigh had recreated a west Belfast shebeen down to the lino on the floor.

Jimmy was variously from Belfast or Monaghan, depending on which of his friends you talked to, and just to be on the safe side he had hired a band for the evening from somewhere between the two. In the corner of the bar, the lead singer, a grey-faced man with matching trousers, was singing rebel ballads to a flock of upturned faces.

In one of the richest, most amnesiac cities on earth, the Irish had gathered to plead poverty and remember.

But in the middle of the noisy throng, there was one silent clue that this was not the old country.

The grey-haired man with cornflower blue eyes sitting at the bar with a pint of Harp beside him was Glenn Barr, the radical commander of the loyalist paramilitary Ulster Defence Association in the Seventies turned Londonderry entrepreneur.

In Toronto on business, he had called into the New Windsor to meet two students from his computer services firm who were in Canada on placement.

Barr may not exactly have been tapping his fingers to the strains of The Boys Behind the Wire, but the sight of him sitting in a bar filled with the noisy battle cries from the ragged edge of constitutional nationalism was one of the more bizarre visions to be had that night in a frozen city.

Three

It was 5.15pm when my train pulled out of Toronto's Union Station on its way to London, where I was to spend three months at the London Free Press daily newspaper as part of an exchange scheme.

It was a sort of Irish exchange scheme, in that nobody was going the other way.

In the sun setting on the mirrored skyscrapers, I left behind a city made of splintered silver and gold against the sky, while on the right cars raced home from Sunday brunch against the steel of Lake Ontario.

Brunch is the Canadian way to spend Sunday, paying around five dollars for the privilege of picking through mounds of food all through the long afternoon as passers-by look in with doleful eyes. Mine earlier that day had taken three hours, and with several local Irish dignitaries there, the conversation tilted inevitably towards the touchstone of the Irish abroad — where in Canada you could get the best pint of Guinness.

"It's McVeigh's right here in Toronto."

"It is not. O'Brien's in Woodstock is the only place."

As I wrote all this down, the train scudded west under a cold and endless sky. In Hyde Park, children tossed baseballs to and fro in swaddled pairs while their parents staged impromptu matches. For some reason the sight made me deeply sad, and for a long time after that I looked out of the window as the train clicked west, unable to speak or write as I tried to work out why.

Finally I thought it just be because I wanted to be down there, wrapping up my baseball mitt and heading home to a timber house with yellow windows and coffee on the stove.

Dear God, if I was this lonely 10 miles out of town, what was I going to be like by the time I got to the Yukon?

But two things cheered me up.

The first was the attendant bringing a free croissant stuffed with ham and cheese, biscuits, and as much coffee as I wanted.

1 thought of the surly ape who had prowled the carriages the last time I travelled on a train in Ireland, dispensing overpriced coffee and mummified sandwiches, and felt much happier.

I felt happier still after I'd read Weekly World News, the paper I'd bought for 80 cents at Union Station from a man whose badly scarred face seemed to left him with an eagerness to please rather than a lifetime of misanthropy.

If I tell you that the top headline on the front page was Loch Ness Monster is Pregnant, you'll get the general picture.

It was one of those papers where the number of exclamation marks after a headline was in inverse proportion to the veracity of the story underneath.

By the time I'd finished it, we were 45 minutes out of Toronto, and all signs of humanity had disappeared.

With the mournful wail of the horn leading the way, the train plunged through black forests, then burst into clearings made ghostly by the rising moon.

I began to think that the attendant, myself and the mathematics student in front of me in the purple baseball cap had become dead men on an imaginary train hurtling towards a station which had ceased to exist.

I began to fall in love with the idea of being dead, and started to understand why it is that some men walk out the door and leave behind them the world of dry rot and rising damp and mortgages, and never come back.

I began to understand why they headed into the vast and empty land out there in the moonlight, with nothing in it. They realised that when there is nothing, everything is possible.

But before the hour was out the signs for Hurley Real Estate and the Savory Electrical Co slid past the window, in which I could once again begin to see the reflections of the mathematics student and the attendant.

And 10 minutes later I too stepped down on to the platform at London, Ontario, a reluctant human being.

Four

I decided to walk to work on my first morning at the Free Press.

I buttoned my coat to halfway up my neck, covered the rest with three layers of scarf, put on a pair of sunglasses to combat snowblindness and piled a woolly hat on top. I looked like Scott of Ontario, and felt like the town idiot.

Fortunately there was no one else on the streets to spot me, and I soon found out why.

I was the only person in London walking to work because I was the only person in London who hadn't listened to the weather forecast this morning.

The weather forecast which had said that it was going to snow, that is. Heavily.

Halfway there I was covered in three inches of freshly fallen and looking like the Abominable Ulsterman.

Except I wasn't even halfway there. I had begun to appreciate the vast distances involved in Canadian travel, and I hadn't even left the city yet.

I think it was about then that I got lost. I know because I met one of the two other men in London who missed the weather forecast this morning.

I first noticed him because he had perfected the unusual art of walking at an angle of 45 degrees to the vertical.

He was also wearing a Stetson, blue jeans and cowboy boots. He looked as if his horse had died five miles back and he hadn't noticed.

"Am I going the right way for York Street?" I yelled at him through the falling flakes.

"No," he said, walking past. Now, I like a man who gets to the point, but just at this minute I needed a little more elaboration.

It finally turned out that I'd been walking parallel to York Street all along. I took a left turn and headed on, trudging past lines of enormous cars swishing past with their air conditioning on and country music on the stereo. I began to develop a pathological hatred of Henry Ford, assuaged by a grimly delightful realisation that the amount of salt on Canadian winter roads puts car driving in the adventure sports league.

I was almost at work, an hour after I'd set out, when I met the only other man in London who hadn't heard the weather forecast that morning.

He was about 104, and was riding his bicycle so slowly that I couldn't quite work out how he kept it upright.

"Boy, will I be glad to get home," he said in a quavering voice as I passed him. I knew how he felt. To hell with the Great Outdoors. Tomorrow I take a cab.

Five

Almost 30 years have gone by since the repeal of the infamous Blue Laws of Ontario, when men and woman drank in separate bars, tavern windows were covered to protect the unsullied populace from the sights inside and you had to sign a chit at City Hall before sneaking your bottle of Seagram's home in a brown paper bag.

But off-licences here, which are still run by the provincial government and called, with commendable accuracy but a depressing lack of imagination, Beer Stores and Liquor Stores, are still full of traps for the unwary.

Try going in and asking for a few bottles of Labatt's, for a start.

"Certainly, sir,' the man behind the counter replied in his well-modulated mid-Ontario accent. "Will that be Labatt's Blue, Blue Light, Genuine Draft, 50, Ice, Crystal or Extra Dry?"

In a panic, you scrabble through your memory for the name of the only other Canadian beer you know — Molson.

"Of course," said Mr mid-Ontario. "Molson Canadian, Canadian Ice, Canadian Light, Dry, Special, Export, Stock Ale, Golden or Old Vienna?"

It's a nightmare scenario which only those who have asked for breakfast in an American diner will understand.

Once you've decided whether you want your eggs brown, white, in an omelette, boiled, three-minute, five-minute, seven-minute, poached, scrambled with or without butter, low-fat or regular margarine, beaten or forked, fried sunny side up, over easy, over medium or over hard, broken yolk or whole yolk, and whether you'd prefer your glass of milk whole, homogenised, pasteurised, one per cent, two per cent, half in half, chocolate, goat or butter, it's almost time for lunch and more ulcer-grinding decisions.

It can only be a matter of time before someone realises that deciding which way to have their eggs and milk in the morning causes American executives more coronaries than the food does.

But anyway, there I was still back in The Beer Store, trying to work out which of the 187 different types of Canadian beer to buy.

The problem was made even more difficult by the fact that there's no beer on display in The Beer Store.

Instead, the walls are lined with empty bottles. It's a bit, I imagine, like going into a brothel and making your choice of girl from a row of lingerie.

It was, unsurprisingly, some time later before I finally decided on my partner for the evening.

"Twelve Sleeman's Cream Ale," Mr mid-Ontario shouted into the gloom, and five seconds later, from the hole in the wall of the cool room next door, slid a slim green and gold 12-pack complete with carrying handle.

It looked like a briefcase for alcoholics.

I gathered it into my arms, and we headed out into the dark and hopeful night, one man and his cold glass harem.

Six

At lunchtime, I walked out into a blizzard and fell into Fatty Patty's, a lovingly recreated Wild West spit and sawdust rib joint near the corner of King and Clarence Street.

Two stuffed chickens were wrestling playfully on the unvarnished wooden wall, and most of the meals involved the premature death of at least one small cow.

It was the sort of place where the standard order was: "Just wipe its hooves and stick it on a plate."

I was waiting for a root beer and nachos supreme without the jalapeño peppers when a young couple came in and sat down at the table opposite.

He was your average high school graduate, but she was Chinese and gorgeous, with her hair in a pony tail.

I felt like going over and saying: "Come away with me. I can give you a better life than this." To the girl, that is.

I was going crazy again. The doctor warned me this would h-happen.

Anyway, I couldn't see her after that, because the waitress brought me a reinforced metal plate with a pile of nachos on it that was seven inches high and a foot across.

I looked at it for a long time before I decided to tackle it the way Hillary had approached Everest: establishing a base camp and working my way up the easiest face.

After 15 minutes of steady eating, I was still only halfway through. Around me, other people had come in, and the waitress was busily staggering from the kitchen with the reinforced plates.

19

Brought back to life, their contents would have taken John Wayne and a good team three days to drive across the Rio Grande.

I finally finished mine, paid the bill, which came to a measly $10.95 — no wonder Canada is in recession — and walked out again into the swirling snow.

There was only one thing that worried me.

I had ordered the medium portion. And since restaurants never advertise what they don't sell, there was someone, somewhere out there who had eaten a large.

Seven

I really should have known better, when someone invited me to a local women's ice hockey match.

In Canada, local means the sort of trip which at home would involve a farewell party and relatives on the front step waving tear-sodden handkerchiefs.

We set off at 1pm. After about an hour, just as I was beginning to realise that this wasn't a jaunt around the block, we passed through Woodstock. Population 29,000, Home of Snow Countess, World's Largest Dairy Producing Cow, And a Great Place to Live proclaimed a series of billboards. By the time I'd finished reading them we were out of Woodstock, so I'm afraid I can't tell you whether it looked like A Great Place to Live after all.

After what seemed like several days, we arrived in Elmira (Home of the World's Biggest Maple Syrup Festival).

It had thawed in Elmira the night before, and at a crossroads a man sat in a black buggy, with the rain pouring down his face and lying on his coat like moonlight on ink. Everything about him was black — his hat, his coat, and the whip which danced over the tail of the black horse which fretted before the buggy, its breath pluming in the cold.

He was a Mennonite, one of a strict Mexican order which speaks only Old German. And you thought Northern Ireland politics was confusing.

Canadian folklore has it that you can tell the strictness of a Mennonite's order by his method of transport; from the black buggy,

21

to the black car with the chrome painted over, to the same car with the chrome showing, right up to the man in the scarlet Cadillac.

But ice skating, it seems, is not an option for them: at the ice rink where the match was to be played, the Elmira citizens finishing the public session were strictly White Anglo-Saxon Protestant parents teaching toddlers to skate with the aid of tiny devices like walking frames.

Around them, one fat man skated faster and faster until the buzzer for the end of the session went and he stopped, as fat as ever but quite out of breath and pleased with himself as the ice hockey players came on.

Deb Van Brenk, the Dutch-Canadian girl who'd brought me here, was the Forest City Rebels goalminder, which involved deliberately placing herself in the way of a piece of hard rubber travelling at up to 60mph. When I'd met her she'd seemed quite sane, which just shows you how reliable appearances are.

The only previous ice hockey match I'd been to was a men's one in Finland, which had consisted of long periods of fighting interrupted by brief spells of hockey.

But in this district, checking — that is, launching yourself at opponents like a human cruise missile — had been banned, which left the players little to do except score goals.

And in these small local leagues, far from the hum of corporate sponsorship, each player was responsible for finding her own backer, which meant that some girls whizzed to and fro silently extolling the virtues of Gro-Pro Lawn Care and Koebel Concrete, while the amateurs hung gloomily behind, their blank shirts untarnished by greed.

In the end, the Rebels beat Elmira 3-0, and I packed up my notebook and headed for the nearest bar thinking what an excellent excuse the victory was for doing a little more research into Canadian beer.

I had a Molson Dry, an Algonquin Draft, a Labatt's 50, a Molson Canadian, a Labatt's Extra Stock, a Molson Old Vienna and a Labatt's Crystal.

And here's what I discovered. It gives me a hangover, just like the stuff back home.

Eight

On Sunday afternoon, there wasn't a whole lot to do for the folks of Middlesex County after they'd had lunch and switched on the dishwasher.

Which is probably why so many of them got into their off-road vehicles and piled on down to the Western Fairgrounds for the annual Forest City wood show.

There, you could buy everything from a rat-tail to a whole house, learn everything you ever wanted to know about varnish, and among the angry buzz of ripsaws and the sweet hum of resin, watch a man with one arm silently carving a tiny bird.

And best of all, you could attend the final of the first annual London belt sander drag racing showdown.

Belt sander drag racing was dreamed up a couple of years ago by a builder in Point Roberts, Washington. It was probably a rainy Sunday afternoon then, too.

The London final consisted of four sanders wired up to an overhead power line belting down a 33ft pine track in pairs, and to say that it was interesting is probably stretching the English language beyond its normal snapping point.

Even to say that the highlight was when one of the sanders crashed halfway down the track is pushing it a bit.

Slightly underwhelmed, I left, covered in a fine film of sawdust, and found myself in the flea market next door, where a sign proclaimed: "Aerobic Vision Power — improve your eyesight in just minutes a day!" next to the Thighmaster stand where the solitary

23

salesman was getting a little frustrated by the average Londoner's lack of interest in their thighs.

"OK, so nobody wants to improve their body, that's all right by me," he sighed wearily.

It was the sort of day where the best place to be was the Laundry Café over on Oxford Street, where couples sat and played Scrabble over a beer as they waited for a red light on the wall to turn yellow and show that their washing had finished.

On the TV in the corner, the Canadian Broadcasting Corporation's evening coverage of the Winter Olympics was just starting.

The CBC's coverage was brought to us by Toyota, a Japanese car company, Diet Coke (Just For The Taste Of It), Molson Canada (What Beer's All About), Royal Bank (Canada's Leader in RSPs), Skor (Discover The Ritual of Rich Milk Chocolate), Esso (You're On Your Way With Us) and Priority Courier (Because Your Priorities Are Ours). It was introduced by Brian William, a man of such glibly patronising insincerity that I wouldn't even buy a new car off him, never mind a used one.

After seven minutes it was interrupted by advertisements of the Olympic sponsors and a trailer for Degrassi Talks, a forthcoming documentary on teenage sexual problems which would be brought to us by Tampax tampons.

I gave up and went back to reading The Great Railway Bazaar, which was brought to me by Paul Theroux.

Outside, the full moon rose at one end of Oxford Street, and the sun sank at the other, at the conclusion of another rainy Sunday in London, Ontario.

And from down by the railroad tracks came the lonely wail of a freight train, heading west faster than a belt sander out of hell.

Nine

It all seemed so simple as I lay in bed that morning at the Rose and Kangaroo. First of all, I was going to be the only person ever to visit Niagara and miss the falls.

Then I was going to drive to Buffalo to try Buffalo Wings and Beef on Weck, that city's twin contributions to heartburn.

And finally, I was going to polish the day off with a spin down to Eden, home of the world's only kazoo factory.

The conversation over breakfast at the Rose of Kangaroo — a Niagara guest house owned by a local woman called Rose and an Australian called Laurie — should have alerted me that the best thing to do that day was to go back to bed with a good book.

There was a woman from Ohio who should have had a Space to Let sign above her head, and her husband, who spent most of the time locked in their room.

The other two couples introduced themselves as Gary and Jennifer, and Hi! and Thelma, down from Toronto for the weekend.

"Uh, well, I think given the choice, I'd drink a whole glass of cream before I'd drink a glass of milk," began Jennifer shyly.

"I must say I prefer it in my coffee. It takes the edge off the bitterness," opined Hi! optimistically.

"I like a nice strong cup of coffee myself," stated Gary conclusively.

I made my excuses and fled into town. On Clifton Hill, the town's main street, honeymoon couples strolled past amusement arcades, wax museums and souvenir shops filled with obese pink pigs, debating which of the Rent a Circular Vibrating Bed for an Hour offers to take up.

Above their heads, a plastic model of the French daredevil Blondin balanced on a tightrope slung between the House of Dracula and the Guinness World of Records.

And above that, the ghost of Oscar Wilde looked down and thought how right he had been when he described Niagara, one of the world's most popular honeymoon destinations, as the second major disappointment of American married life.

I got into the office car and headed south for Buffalo. In my rear-view mirror, the heavy industries of New York State emptied the contents of their corporate bladder into Canada with a great roar of relief, and Japanese tourists flitted to and fro in the polluted mist.

In their opaque yellow capes, they looked like a tiny doomed species of moth for whom endlessly taking photographs of each other was the only hope of survival.

Buffalo had to be better.

Buffalo wasn't.

Buffalo is the home of the only two mail order houses left standing in America. Sold by Sears and Roebuck for £2,000 in the Twenties, they're still lived in.

The price included everything but the kitchen sink, which is where the catchphrase came from.

Buffalo is also the home of Frank and Teressa Bellissimo's Anchor Bar, where Buffalo Wings were invented on a dark and stormy night in 1964 when all Teressa had left in the kitchen when a bunch of starving customers rolled in was a pile of chicken wings fit only for soup stock.

She fired them up, smothered them in spicy sauce, and served them with celery and blue cheese dip, and hey presto, the rest is hysteria. Or listeria, if you don't heat them enough.

The wings are eaten with your fingers. Which means they get covered in hot sauce. Which means you'd be well advised to wash your hands before you to go the toilet. Believe me.

Believe me, too, when I say Buffalo was so dull that they close the shops on a Saturday. Even the tourist office had shut up shop, leaving only a dripping sign outside proclaiming that Millard

26

Fillmore, one of the USA's less memorable presidents, had lived there from 1858 until his death in 1874. Of boredom, I imagine.

Let me put it another way. Mel, the black man I gave a lift into town, was regretting leaving the US Army because they'd threatened to post him to Alaska. Compared to Buffalo, the company of caribou beckoned like endless cocktail parties.

I dropped him off and went in search of Eden, the village south of Buffalo which is the home of the world's only kazoo factory and museum, established in 1907.

The kazoo, the only original American instrument, was invented in the 1840s, and now has 15,000 bands devoted to it, including a classical ensemble called Kazoophony.

Sadly, for this part of the trip I'd picked up as my navigator a fellow Omagh man called Dominic McClements who was even worse at giving directions than I was at receiving them.

If you've never driven around rural New York State in the pouring rain looking in vain for the world's only kazoo factory, you've never appreciated how close it is possible to come to the edge of sanity.

At 4.45pm, 15 minutes before the factory was due to close, I stopped at a garage and persuaded the owner to let me use his phone so I could get through to the kazoo factory and persuade the caretaker to stay a little longer.

But by the time Dominic and I got there it was 5.20, she had gone, and I had added the world's only
kazoo factory to the list of Great Tourist Attractions I Have Missed, along with Heidelberg Castle and the 10.30 bus to Liechtenstein.

Through the windows of the pale yellow clapboard building, rows of kazoos lay along the shelves, and in the factory at the back, piles of metal ones lay gleaming in baskets. I had failed to fall for Niagara, and been bored by Buffalo.

But missing the world's only kazoo factory was the worst of all.

I pressed my face to the window as the rain streamed down, and felt like a child locked for ever out of the toyshop of dreams.

Ten

New York State, on a Sunday evening.

In the Press Box bar on Niagara Street, Niagara, men whose waistlines are tributes to a lifetime of burgers and beer hunker down for more of the same.

Occasionally one of them will shuffle to his feet to feed quarters into the slot in the jukebox by the side of which the owner has pasted a sign saying No Loonies. This is not a reference to the sanity of his customers, but to the traditional nickname of the Canadian dollar coin, which has a loon on the reverse.

Outside, as the jukebox cranks itself up for Frank Sinatra's fourth rendition this evening of New York, New York, the litter bins bulge with battered training shoes, shopping bags and crumpled receipts.

And in the street beyond, the queue of Canadian cars stretches around the corner for over a mile to the Rainbow Bridge which will take them back across the river into Canada.

In every car, the occupants are wearing brand new clothes and shoes, and brightly guilty expressions which they hope will get them through the Nothing to Declare lines.

And behind them they leave the rustle of closing tills and a sigh of all-American satisfaction as the sun goes down on another shopping Sunday.

Cross-border shopping is something that Canadian shoppers love, and Canadian shops hate.

Shops hate it because it loses them an estimated $3.5 billion annually, and 55,000 jobs. Critics in the government claim that the five million Canadians who go shopping across the border every month are killing Canada's economy and endangering the welfare system which higher taxes are necessary to pay for.

Shoppers retort that the government created cross-border shopping by accepting a free trade agreement with the US, maintaining artificially high prices on groceries and imposing the hated seven per cent Goods and Services Tax, aka GST, or Government Sucks Tax, as Canadians have fondly christened it.

In Ontario, where the provincial government tacks on an extra eight per cent Provincial Sales Tax, the complaints are so loud that they almost drown out Frank Sinatra.

But not quite.

I drain my beer, take an admiring glance at my new Timberland loafers, check my innocent expression in the mirror, and join the queue for the Rainbow Bridge.

Eleven

I never knew ice could be so enjoyable without something around it.

Yes, I've been skiing, and the time has come to apologise to all the friends I lambasted for being yuppies when they packed their C& A ski suits and headed off for a week in Kitzbühel.

Sliding down a frozen slope with a pair of planks strapped to your feet is, I'm afraid to say, everything it's cracked up to be.

Who would have thought it when I presented myself to ace London Ski Club instructor Jana Tichy, who was going to transform me into Jean-Claude Whatsisname for a mere $29 plus $9 equipment rental?

For my $9 I had been furnished with a pair of boots which made me walk like I'd been drinking all night. Now, normally it costs me a lot more than $9 to walk like that, so I wasn'et complaining.

I also got a pair of skis which were about to attached to the boots by a mysterious process which Jana, a tanned Czechoslovakian who was wearing sunglasses, was going to reveal to me.

Jana wasn't wearing the sunglasses because of the snow, but because I was clothed in the only waterproof clothes I could find in the apartment I was staying in: a pair of neon pink ski socks with turquoise stripes, bright yellow cycling dungarees with a rip at the crotch and a blue nylon anorak. I looked like Albania's first yuppie.

I clumped out onto the snow behind Jana, attached my boots to my skis by a process which I'm not going to tell you unless you send me $9, and looked up mournfully at the two-year-olds skiing down the beginners' slope backwards at 120mph.

Jana laid an understanding hand on my arm.

"It's never too late to learn," she said. She was right.

First of all she taught me to walk sideways up the slope. I felt like a crab with crabs, but I didn't fall over.

Then she showed me to slide forwards and stop by snowploughing, which is a technical term I'm prepared to discuss for a further $9.

But I still hadn't fallen over! Good heavens, was I destined to become skiing's first 35-year-old child prodigy?

Well, you know what they say about pride. By this stage Jana decided I was ready for the ski-tow, which involves grabbing a metal handle and being pulled to the top of the hill, then stepping off.

I was doing fine until the stepping off bit. That was when I became the only skier ever to fall down going up.

To add injury to insult, the next handle gave me a whack on the head, raising a bump which did nothing for my streamlining.

Undeterred, I spent the next two hours learning how to turn and zooming down the slope faster and faster. I even beat a couple of two-year-olds.

In fact, I thought as I went to hand my skis back, I want to be reborn as a little Norwegian boy and learn to ski before I can walk.

"Great fun, isn't it?" I said to the man standing by the hire desk.

"I recognise that accent," said the man, who turned out to be called Arnold Owens. "Are you a Tyrone man?"

"Norwegian," I said.

"You can't fool me," said Arnold, "my mother was from Fivemiletown."

Twelve

The weather had a clearance sale on the day of my second skiing lesson.

In the morning, the ski club cancelled all its lessons because it was 13 above and the snowmaking machine wouldn't work.

Then, that night, the cold front hit.

Now, at home a cold front means throwing another bucket of coal on the fire. Here, it means the
bucket sticks to your hand.

It means sitting in a downtown bar looking out through the double-glazed windows at a scene from Dante's Refrigerator, as snow howls down the street outside.

A man came in wearing a coonskin hat, opening a tiny window into the past, when the pioneers of
100 years ago struggled through winters like this in dugout cabins with sod roofs and no windows.

Other people stumbled in through the swing doors, their faces frozen into the expressions they had left home with.

They brought wild rumours about the temperature, sending it tumbling as fast as the snow outside. It was 28 below, said one woman. No, it was 40 below with the wind chill factor, said a man. It was going to get worse before it got better, said another. The only thing to do was to sit tight and have a beer, said a fourth, making more sense than the other three put together.

Suddenly I saw a warm front approaching. It belonged to the waitress. I ordered a beer, and told her to make sure it was a cold one.

The next morning, all was still.

The train to Toronto was filled with the voices of children, like tiny, clear streams trickling slowly towards the lake of being grown up.

"Daddy, what's that funny train over there?"

"It's a snowplough."

"Does it clear away the snow for all the other trains?"

"Yes."

Outside, the only way to describe the snow was to say it was deep and crisp and even. The whole effect was serenely beautiful. For anyone on the train who cared to look, it was a Christmas morning of the soul, and they had just been handed life as a present.

In the carriage down the end, the conductor and his assistant were talking railroads.

"I don't think I can trade off. If you're regular road you can, but if you're regular yard you can't."

"No, they changed that last year so yard can. Did you sign on under the old 1314?"

"Yup. Have a copy here, if you want to have a look at it."

The inspection of the old 1314 was interrupted by a middle-aged man in rust-coloured trousers who wanted to know where the bathroom was.

"'Mixed is left down there, men's is right," said the conductor.

"Mixed?"

"They got more rights'n we do," said the assistant conductor.

"Naw, that's not it. They did a survey, and they just go to the bathroom more," said the conductor.

"And spend more time while they're at it," said the assistant. The three of them shared out a little laughter.

Five minutes later, the conductor collected the breakfast trays, dropping a wrapper. The man in the rust trousers, coming back from the mixed bathroom, picked it up. In Canada, everyone is in charge of litter.

"Say," he said to the conductor, "you didn't by any chance work in the yard up at Ottawa?"

"Sure did."

''Know my dad, Slattery?"

"Slattery in electrics?"

"That's him. And Hoogie."

"Old Bogies Hoogie. And Schmidt."

"Sure. Schmidt in welding."

"Well, I'll be."

And so the train trundled on towards Toronto, as the conductor and the assistant conductor and the man in the rust trousers talked about Bogies Hoogie and the old 1314, and the children looked out at the snow, deep and crisp and even, and hoped that it would always be like this.

Thirteen

Saint Patrick's Day in Toronto started with a crisis that would have tried the patience of the man himself.

Clutching a hangover the size of Kerry and feeling green about the gills after a night of drowning 40 shades of shamrock, a ragged collection of us staggered through the biting cold to a nearby public house.

Now, on most evenings of the week this particular hostelry was the scene of much weeping and gnashing of teeth over the attractions of the old country by a bunch of people who after a couple of pints of stout had forgotten that when they were in the old country they couldn't wait to get out of it.

But on this particular bright and sunny morning, the chief attraction of the establishment was a full Irish breakfast, which consisted of as much cholesterol as you could handle for a mere $7.50.

We ordered at 10.30am. Sadly, the kitchen was running on Irish time for the day. At 11.30 a discreet inquiry in the general direction of the waitress elicited the information that the chef was struggling with the difficulties of cooking for 50 on a single frying pan.

After that, without any further prompting, the waitress became an expert at keeping the increasingly ravenous masses up to date on the state of play vis a vis the chances of getting food in their bellies that day, or any other.

After another hour had passed, she could well have got a job as one of those television people who stand in front on the Kremlin holding a microphone and muttering with grim professionalism: "Well, Simon, as I stand here, the latest news from behind me is..."

At 35 minutes past noon, she informed us that the stove had broken down. By one, the chef had followed suit and the second scullery maid had taken over.

At a quarter past, a single steaming plate of rashers, sausages, black and white pudding, eggs, soda bread and potato bread was borne triumphantly from the kitchen.

Fifty starving stomachs watched in awe as it was carried to the table of a bearded man in the corner who had been there since dawn. As it was placed before him, he toyed briefly with the notion of raffling it for a sum which would have placed him in comfortable retirement, before tucking in with the aid of a fork and one of the several knives which were by then protruding from his back.

Time passed. The jacket of the man sitting next to me went slowly out of fashion.

The rest of us began to hallucinate. At the next table, a couple who seemed to have come in with no children suddenly had two. The kids grew up, went to the bar when they reached 18, and eventually began talking nostalgically of the day their parents had ordered breakfast.

Finally, the grand-daughter of the waitress who had originally taken our order emerged from the kitchen with our food. Thankfully, she ignored inflation and let us pay at the original price.

We ate it, placed our order for next year, and staggered replete into the street, fully expecting to see the latest model Ford cruise silently overhead.

Surprisingly, it was still the same afternoon, and the Saint Patrick's Day parade was drawing to a close over on Richmond Street.

A collection of frostbitten colleens danced past, watched by mystified children wearing green noses. They were followed by a procession of lorries representing each of the counties, bearing stuffed donkeys, ceilidh bands, entire thatched cottages and post offices, and a man in a grass skirt who was later taken away suffering from cultural confusion.

On the building across the street, the digital thermometer read 15 below, and my ballpoint pen finally froze solid.

It began to snow as County Antrim trundled past in a pickup truck, watched up an Italian policeman on an American motorcycle.

I put away my notebook, decided to go home, and then realised that I hadn't a clue where it was.

Fourteen

Caroline is charming and beautiful as she sits chatting intelligently about every subject under the sun at a Toronto bar.

She is also naked.

Caroline is one of half a dozen table dancers at the bar in Yonge Street, which is as close as Toronto gets to Sin City.

In return for a smile from any of the men who wander into the bar at all hours of the day, she will sit chatting for five minutes if she doesn't like them, or 15 minutes if she does.

Then, for $5, she will bring over a little wooden dais, step daintily up on it, and perform a little erotic dance as she slowly removes her clothes.

But she is so charming, and has convinced her temporary patron so successfully that they are the best of friends, that he normally spends most of the time looking into her eyes rather than where he thinks he paid his money for.

And since this is Canada, vulgarity is out of the question. The atmosphere as Caroline, Sabrina or any of the half dozen other girls peel off their clothes is more like a nude garden party than a sleazy strip joint.

They are on first name terms with most of the men who line the mirrored stage for the show every 15 minutes to hug their bottles of Labatt's Blue and exchange pleasantries. But although prostitution is legal and increasingly common on Yonge Street, they will not go home with customers.

"Hey, Jack, how you doing today? You like my new outfit?" says Sabrina as she waltzes on stage past a discreet notice asking the customers not to touch the dancers.

"I love it, take it off," says Jack, to laughter all around.

To all appearances, the girls are also on good terms with each other.

"You have to be," says Caroline. "I've worked in places where the girls hated each other if one got more dances than the rest, and it was just misery every day.

"But here we help each other out, or get together and have a word with any guy who's drunk or as little out of line.

"I like dancing here. The guys who come in are nice, and it's not too heavy."

She grew up with foster parents north of Toronto, and wanted to put her exceptional looks to use as a fashion model when she was at high street.

"But I wasn't tall enough. You have to be about 18ft tall for fashion. So a friend suggested this. The first time I did it I was so nervous I wouldn't even take off my top. Oh boy! But I like my body, and I like the fact that the guys like it."

She earns $450 a week, and pays $1040 a month for an apartment two blocks away which she shares with her boyfriend and a cat called Fred.

"No, he doesn't mind me dancing. In fact, he comes in some nights. One night l danced for him, and this guy came up to him afterwards and said: 'Hey, I think she likes you, you know that?' We laughed all the way home at that one."

Since this is a Saturday, she has tomorrow off. In a city ruled for much of this century by immigrant Orangemen from Ulster and Scotland, sex still stops for Sunday.

"Well, listen, you make sure and enjoy the rest of the weekend. It's been a pleasure talking to you," says Caroline, shaking my hand politely.

She goes away to put on her clothes, and five minutes later steps out into Yonge Street. Although it is one in the morning, she feels perfectly safe walking home through the well-lit streets of the city they still call Toronto the Good.

Home to her boyfriend, and a cat called Fred.

I drained my beer and walked out into Yonge Street, where almost immediately I was approached by a large black man in a leather jacket. I steeled myself for the worst and prepared to warn him that I had a black belt in origami.

"I'm sorry to bother you," he said pleasantly, "but can you tell me what time it is?"

I told him, and was looking in a baffled manner at a poster for a Wolfe Tone concert in the Hungarian Centre when a blind man tapped me on the shoulder.

"Can you spare a dime, a dollar, a nickel or a quarter?" he sang.

"Sorry, no change," I lied. What I actually meant was that it was too cold to take my hands out of my pockets.

I decided to walk another couple of hundred yards. It was lucky I didn't decide to walk to the end of the street, since Yonge Street runs out of the city all the way to James Bay, 1,190 miles away.

On the way back I met the blind man again. He recognised the sound of my footsteps before I spoke.

"Still no change, eh?" he said.

I gave him a dollar for being so darned clever, and went back to my hotel room. I had spent a day in Toronto, seen the world and become an expert on the city.

Everyone is an expert on Toronto after their first day there. It takes a second day to become a beginner.

Fifteen

Being in a strange country makes even walking to work in the morning exciting.

Look, there are people who've left their cars in the driveway with the engine running to warm up while they have breakfast!

Try doing that in west Belfast, and your Golf GTI would be wrapped around a lamp post before the toast had popped.

And a beautifully constructed snow castle in someone's front garden, with the house number engraved beside the drawbridge.

And the railroad tracks. I lay awake last night listening to the long mournful wail of the freight trains heading west, and now I know where it came from.

And a school playground, looking like a bag of allsorts with all the bright outdoor clothes.

And a parking sign outside an office saying: "Reserved — Catton and Tuttle."

What happens when Catton and Tuttle turn up at the same time? Fisticuffs in the parking lot and blood on the snow, I shouldn't wonder.

And a lawyer's office called Little, Reeves, Mahoney, Jarrett and Harte. Just think, if Reeves, Mahoney, Jarrett and Harte agreed to take their names off, they could save millions in the amount of time their secretaries spent introducing the firm on the phone, and they could all take a cut of the profits.

And all this because I took a different way to work this morning, down Maitland instead of Colborne, until I got to the Free Press, which is at York and Colborne. I love the way Canadians give addresses like that, with the street and the nearest cross street. It gives me a thrill even writing it down.

And it gives me a thrill, too, to walk down avenues sparkling with snow and ice and newness. It must be what the Queen feels like on royal visits, always arriving in a world which still smells of fresh paint.

By the way, Your Majesty, useful Canadian phrases to know in winter and summer are: "Cold enough for you, eh?" and: "Hot enough for you, eh?" They can be reversed if irony is what you're after.

However, although Canadian English is a lot closer to the real thing than the American sort, it still contains unexpected traps for the unwary.

Arranging a lift to an ice hockey match, I got an extremely strange look from my potential chauffeuse when I asked her what time she was picking me up.

It transpired that I was asking her something that young men do not ask young ladies when they've barely been introduced.1 should have asked her when she was calling over.

I think she's getting the hang of it, though. She came up to me today and said: "Do you want me to pick you over on Saturday?"

"Why don't you run me up instead?" I told her.

I got another blank look later when I told someone else that the phone was engaged. "What, to another phone?" she said.

Mind you, I should have been alerted when on my first morning in work, a strapping chap walked up, shook my hand, and said: "Hi. I'm randy!"

Who says Canadians don't have a sense of humour?

Sixteen

Thirty-five years old, and never hired a car. Good heavens, what can I have been thinking of?

Money, that's what. When I needed a car for the weekend, the rental company down the road quoted me $89, which sounded too good to be true.

That's probably because it was.

After they'd added the collision waiver, the Goods and Services Tax, the Provincial Sales Tax, the petrol tax, the tyre wear tax, the extra mileage penalty and the tax for breathing, the total came to $181.20.   For that I got a — hold on, I can't remember what it was. It was one of those cars you forget the moment you stop looking at it.

I headed east out of town in my Blandmobile, loaded down with taxes as I drove past streets named by someone with same imagination as the man who had designed my car — First Street, Second Street and Third Street.

Then I got to Crumlin and saw signs for London Airport. I didn't know where the hell I was. I was lost, and I was worrying about money. I felt like crying. But I didn't. This was the land where bawling was for babies.

Finally I got onto Highway 401, a bumpy, winter-ravaged road filled with big truckers hogging the fast lane and refusing to shift over.

Except in Canada there is no fast lane. There's a slow lane, and a slower one. The highway speed limit is 100kmh, or 62mph, and that's just what everyone sits at, with the cruise control and air conditioning on, Bryan Adams on the stereo and the five litre engine thinking: "What's the point of it all?"

Now, I'm no road hog, but if I want to drive at 100mph until I'm stopped by an officer of the law and have to explain to him that it's an emergency because I don't like Bryan Adams, then I wish Canadian drivers would move over and let me do it.

In fact, I only saw one police car. It was sitting by the roadside with no one in it. Both drivers had obviously died of old age waiting for a Canadian to drive past at 63mph.

I gave up trying to pass the truckers, put some good old rock and roll on the radio, and tried to figure out how to switch on the cruise control.

But then how would I switch it off?

It was worrying about shooting off the edge of Newfoundland at a steady 62mph that made me miss the turnoff for Niagara and left me heading towards Toronto. I pulled in at a service station in the middle of nowhere and walked up to the manager, a dark-haired man who introduced himself as Glenn Robinson.

"I'm coming from London and trying to get to Niagara," I said.

"London, England, or London, Ontario?"

"Both, but Belfast, originally. I'm a journalist there."

"Oh? My cousin's a journalist in Belfast. Guy called Grattan."

"You mean Gary Grattan from the Belfast Telegraph?"

"That's him. Maybe you could give him a baseball hat from me."

I give up. The world's so small that there's no point going anywhere.

Seventeen

A grim disease is sweeping across Canada; worse than the smallpox and measles which wiped out hundreds of thousands of Indians, worse than the gold fever which sent men to an icy grave in the Yukon.

It originated in the USA, and there is no known cure.

Yes, it's the chronic inability of sales assistants to avoid saying: "Have a nice day" as they hand over the change.

Nice? Nice? I can't think of anything worse than having a nice day. You might as well wish that someone got up, put on a pinstripe suit with a matching tie and pocket handkerchief, then had watery porridge for breakfast, followed by eight hours filling in forms at the office, a return home to a lukewarm bath, a soap opera on TV and a medium-strength beer before bedtime in separate beds.

Nice? Pah! I'd much rather leave a shop with these words ringing in my ears: "Have the sort of day where you're sacked by the boss and decide to hitch to the Arctic, marry a polar bear and live in a two-storey igloo."

Or the sort of day where the prime minister announces that Canada has declared war on Florida, and every able-bodied man in the country has to report to his local army base for fitting with a black leather jacket and floral Bermuda shorts by teatime.

Or the sort of day where your wife announces that she's running off with a Hare Krishna to spend the rest of her life in Tibet humming mantras and rearing killer goats, leaving you free to buy a

Harley Davidson Electraglide and roar off to Patagonia, picking up sweet-natured cowgirls as you go.

That's the sort of day we want, folks! Exciting and different! To hell with nice!

Eighteen

Following in the wake of the Have a Nice Day syndrome, another phenomenon is creeping across the border from the United States — the Incredible Exploding People.

In the USA, gross obesity is practically compulsory among certain sections of the middle-aged middle classes, caused by a daily intake of food which would keep an average African township going for a year. A secondary symptom is a complete lapse of good taste, forcing the sufferer to wear clothes which would be better reserved for those still on viewing terms with their feet.

The Calvinistic Canadians have so far resisted the tendency to explode, but while dawdling through the aisles of my local Cal-U-Mart the other day, idly pondering such conundrums as what exactly Homo Milk was and whether I should choose the honey and garlic or the teriyaki sausages from the deli, I came face to face with an Incredible Exploding Woman, pushing a trolley with a quantity of provisions which would have got Scott and his entire expedition back safely from the Antarctic.

The mounds of flesh above her neck, which would have done credit to one of those Chinese dogs with a skin four sizes too large for them, were only held in place by a pair of batwing glasses for which Dame Edna Everage would have gladly pawned a favourite frock or two.

In the middle of this gratuitous ensemble of skin and plastic, the Lord had chosen in a moment of whimsical despair to plonk a tiny, ludicrous cupid's bow of a mouth which its owner had endowed generously with orange lipstick. Somewhere in the shadowy recesses above, I caught a hint of matching eye shadow.

Pausing only for a fleeting glimpse of black plastic shoes, red nylon ski pants and an overcoat apparently made of dried milk, I fled into the open air clutching my sugar-free muesli, a reconfirmed aesthete.

Nineteen

So enthralled was I by my first skiing lesson a while back that when fellow journalists Richard Sheriff and Dominic McClements came up from Niagara Falls for the weekend from their placements on weekly papers there, I persuaded the gullible fools during a spell of drinking on Saturday night that I could teach them to ski on Sunday.

The next morning, too stupid to say we were only joking, we dug a set of bright yellow cycling waterproofs out of the cupboard under the stairs, and tossed coins to see who got to wear them.

Dominic won — and instantly regretted it, since they made him look a district council workman looking for a hole to fill in.

After they'd got over the first half hour of falling over, they were delighted with themselves. In fact,
Dominic was so ecstatic the first time he slid all the way down that he forget to stop.

Slightly bruised by the gable of the clubhouse but undaunted, he soldiered on until he had opened a rip in the right leg of the trousers from crotch to ankle which ballooned out on every descent until he was forced to aim himself at the side of the hill and describe a wide circle all the way to the other side at the bottom.

All of which he did with commendable accuracy before I gave up and taught him how to steer. But then, us Ulstermen are noted for our ingenuity.

As for me, I was so proud of my transition from novice to fully qualified ski coach that I hit the slopes again last night, and managed to plummet from the top of the advanced slope, scaring myself witless but arriving in one piece.

I mentioned this with droll insouciance to one of the staff in the clubhouse, and received the response that she'd been doing that slope when she was five years old.

In fact, she got so bored with it that she and her little friends used to change places in the chair lift 50ft above the ground, ski down holding hands in a spinning circle, and then top it off by waiting until the club had turned off the floodlights and skied down in total darkness.

Oh well. Deciding to put off turning professional for a week or two, I went to London's Grand Theatre to see a play called Warriors, about two advertising men trying frantically to think up a new slogan for the Canadian armed forces.

It was memorable, but only for about five minutes.

Upstairs in the bar afterwards, I met some of the people involved in the London theatre scene. I could tell they were artistic because one of them was wearing a cape, two scarves and a professional expression of bright-eyed interest in everything around him.

The rest were using gestures as if they were going out of style first thing in the morning, and miming as they spoke. "Fractured his leg? Good heavens!"

"Well no, actually, it was just a scratch. A mere bee sting, in fact, barely broke the skin."

One in the corner was muttering: "Kurosawa's Throne of Blood? Mmm, bit too heavy even for an adaption of Macbeth. The Upanishads were a lot cooler."

I fled home and checked my ears for hairs, just in case I was getting old or something.

Twenty

I could tell it was going to be one of those days when Ed ordered a brandy for breakfast. Of course, it had all been his idea in the first place, when he suggested a tour of the unsung highlights of south western Ontario.

Like the migrating tundra swans at Long Point, the tobacco kilns around Sparta, and the grand-daddy of them all, the best mess of perch and celery bread in the world at the Erie Beach Hotel in Port Dover.

Our guides for the day were Ed, the Free Press' Deputy Travel Editor, Doug the Travel Editor, and Bruce, a senior feature writer, and as I look back on that Saturday now, all I see is a series of bright vignettes of the sort that are supposed to pass before a drowning man in his final moments.

I see, for example, one and a half thousand tundra swans sitting on a lake and nibbling corn as they take a break on their 4,000-mile journey from Chesapeake Bay to Alaska, and I hear Bruce, our driver, saying to Ed, our navigator: "Lucky you're not a swan, Ed, or they'd be in Patagonia by now."

Ed, a man who hath no greater love than this, that he would lay down his sanity for an appalling pun, retorts by accusing Bruce of trying to steal his tundra.

The next image of the sunspilt day takes place in a rural bar somewhere near the Quaker hamlet of Sparta, where the ochre, white and green tobacco kilns stretch across the fields like holiday cottages.

In this bar there is a tiny, yapping dog owned by an enormous, silent barman who hands out bottles from behind the counter, since there is no draught beer.

Ed, Doug and Bruce are recalling Ontario's infamous Blue Laws, which meant that until 1963 unescorted men and women had to drink in separate bars. Singing and carrying beer between tables was banned, and bar windows were painted over so the unsullied populace could not see the unparalleled depths to which humanity had sunk inside.

Bruce was fondly recalling leading a chorus of When Irish Eyes Are Smiling in front of a bar owner who didn't know what to do, since he was breaking the law but making money at the same time. Not that Bruce cared — between verses he was busy chatting up a sweet young Irish girl called Mary Murphy who, although he didn't recognise her immediately, was his future wife.

After Bruce has fondly recalled this, Ed fondly recalls that Bruce missed the last turning. A violent argument is about to ensue, when everyone realises that all this talk of the Blue Laws has made them thirsty.

"God, this is the first time I've been drunk in the afternoon for years," says Doug. "It's like making love in the kitchen."

When the journey resumes, Ed points out that we are approaching the world's only official turtle crossing.

"I know," says Bruce. "We've just passed a Shell station."

But Ed is plotting his revenge. As we disembark outside the Erie Beach Hotel in Port Dover, Bruce foolishly voices the opinion that the bright star creeping into the evening sky is the Dog Star.

"Are you sirius?" says Ed, quick as a comet.

At last we bid the old-timers farewell back in London, tell Ed he was right about the celery bread, and go out drinking. Like we need it.

At some stage in the evening, we find ourselves in a lap dancing bar at which the main attraction is the appearance of Miss Nude New Brunswick, who is so stunning that I make a mental note to get myself to New Brunswick as soon as possible.

By the time we emerge, full of beer and a newfound love for New Brunswick, it is two on the Sabbath morn.

"I'm starving," says Richard.

"Me too," said Dominic.

"We'll be lucky to find anything open at this time of night," I say, until miraculously we round a corner and find a Wendy's 24-Hour Drive-In.

There is only one problem. At this time of night, it won't serve us on foot. You drive up to an intercom in a wall, give your order, then drive around to a serving hatch to collect it.

Suddenly a brilliant idea flashes across my mind, dazzling in its simplicity.

So it is that 30 seconds later we find ourselves beside Wendy's intercom, pretending to be a car. I am driving, Richard is in the passenger seat doing an excellent impersonation of a V8, and Dominic, for some reason, is sitting in the middle of the bonnet.

"Dominic, get inside the car or you'll freeze to death," says Richard.

With Dominic safely in the back seat and Richard starting the engine again, we give our order. I have to shout, because of the laughter from the actual car behind us — although the driver, caught in the grip of our imagination, is leaving a good boot's length behind Dominic.

Finally we get to the serving hatch.

"Uh, where's your car?" says the girl, clutching our burgers suspiciously.

"It broke down around the corner," says Richard innocently, as I collect the burgers and we walk home, munching contentedly.

And the next morning, the car is still not there, exactly where we didn't leave it.

Very honest people, these Canadians.

Part Two

The West

Twenty-one

The woman sitting in the waiting room of London train station was quite beautiful, and quite mad. She was stuffing sweets into her mouth, but they tumbled out as fast as she could force them in.

Between mouthfuls, she sang: "The day they came to hang me high was the day they brought me roses."

Two men sat looking at her. One was black, wearing neon green sunglasses and a black shirt with a white collar, and the other was almost completely covered in hair. I sat and looked at the three of them. If things are like this before I even leave the station, I thought, maybe I should have stayed in bed today.

But there was no going back now. In 20 minutes, I would take the train to Toronto, and tonight I would leave on a month-long adventure which will take me across the great prairies, then north to Dawson City, home of the Klondike gold rush, and south across the Rocky Mountains to Vancouver. I was travelling light: just a change of shirts, a Swiss Army knife, a bottle of beer. And a three-foot zip. If I got really cold, I'd strangle a polar bear, take out the wet bits, sew the zip up the back, and hey presto — a polar bear suit. It'd come in handy for shopping trips when I went back to Belfast. Two raw seals, dear, and don't argue about the change.

Perhaps it was best that by the time I got to Toronto Station the madwoman, the priest and the werewolf were nowhere to be seen. Instead, the first-class departure lounge was mostly filled with elderly couples apparently traumatised by the fact that they'd got this far in life and couldn't afford the plane. Caught between the failures queuing outside for second-class seats, and the successes sipping whisky far above in the clouds, they shuffled towards their sleeping compartments, and I tagged along behind, hoping I never got that ungrateful to ride on one of the world's great train journeys – coast to coast on The Canadian, the gleaming silver train which had been beautifully restored by VIA Rail, the national network.

A whole month with nothing to do but travel, think and write. Good heavens, 1 couldn't think of anything better.

I found my two-berth compartment, then stuck my head into the corridor to find an enormous man trundling towards me, pushing a bow wave of body odour before him. I stepped back and held my breath in case he uttered the dreaded words: "Is this 122B?"

But he passed on, breathing heavily. In his turgid wake bobbed fragments of Old Spice, garlic, stale Cheddar sandwiches and beer.

Giddy with relief, I took my solitary bottle to the domed observation car at the back of the train, and watched as the great silver spine of The Canadian snaked out of Toronto, the single eye of its headlights gouging out the night.

By the time the train's glittering skin had finally sloughed off the lights of the city, all the passengers had gone to bed. Except for the enormous, malodorous man, who I squeezed past in the corridor on my way back.

He was gazing out of the window, north towards Sudbury, a landscape so lunified by nickel mining that the American astronauts trained there for the Apollo landings.

But there was no moon tonight, and all he could see in the window was his own reflection, surrounded by a wavering halo of ancient cheese.

Twenty-two

After breakfasting famously on scrambled eggs and ham, the occupants of The Canadian dashed to the observation cars, sat down, pressed the record button on their Sony handycams — and read the newspapers.

Outside, passing before their very headlines, was a sunsplit vista of forest and snow, of silver birch and shadowed valleys dipping into the frozen muskeg of northern Ontario — the terrifying swamps which provided the first great challenge to the men who built the Canadian Pacific Railway transcontinental line between 1880 and 1885.

Wooden piles 100ft long rammed into these swamps failed to touch bottom. They swallowed thousands of tons of gravel, miles of fresh track and, on several occasions, entire locomotives which took their engineers and stokers with them to a viscous, watery grave.

But worse was to come.

The first time this section of track was used in earnest was in April 1885, when 3,324 troops were moved west by train to quell the Saskatchewan rebellion and save the tottering CPR from bankruptcy. As manager Cornelius Van Horne shrewdly realised, the government could not fail to bail out a company which had helped it fight the rebellion.

But for the soldiers, the journey was to be worse than any war. Because sections of the track had not yet been equipped with passenger carriages, they travelled in open cars in temperatures of -20C, soaked by snow and rain at night as they tried in vain to sleep. By day, their faces were blistered and scorched beyond recognition, and the glare off the ice blinded many, leaving their eyes feeling as if they had been sandpapered and their world a red, shimmering blur.

On sections where the track had not been laid at all, they marched for up to 40 miles through slush up to their knees, taking six hours to cover 10 miles and often falling unconscious into snowdrifts by the side of the track.

At one stage Captain A. Hamlyn Todd of the Government-General's Foot Guards counted 40 exhausted men lying in the snow, many of them face down with their colleagues too tired to lift them. And even when they got to the next section of track, they had to wait up to 17 hours for the next train. Several went mad with the cold. By the time they finally got to Red Rock and collapsed into covered carriages for the unbroken ride to Qu'Appelle, many had not slept for over 50 hours.

Compared to that, I hesitate to say, 107 years on, that all I had to cope with were VIA Rail's taps.

Last night the hot one ran cold, and the cold hot. This morning both were cold, and by lunchtime both were lukewarm. The rate of flow, meanwhile, depended entirely on the speed of the train. At full tilt I could wash two shirts, but when we stopped at stations a sock was quite beyond me.

At teatime, the conductor announced mysteriously that we would be stopping for half an hour at Hornepayne, which is halfway between nowhere and nowhere else.

Everyone decamped to the G & L Variety Store to buy food, since trains seem to encourage the siege mentality in people.

Having already stocked up with bread and cheese in Toronto, I found myself outside the Packsack, a tottering retail outlet high on a hill, inside which could be dimly seen stone steps, old romantic novels, metal toy cars and a wall lined with the faded covers of Patton's knitting patterns.

It looked just like Pat Rafferty's in Carrickmore, where my mother used to take me on Saturday morning shopping trips. I pressed my nose against the glass door, trying to see if I was in there, in the gobstopper gloom, but from down the hill came the cry of: "All aboard!" and I traipsed reluctantly back to adulthood. And so to dinner, where I found myself sharing a table with Fred, Eva and Luther.

Fred and Eva were from Reno, Nevada. After visiting Skagway in Alaska on holiday, they had fallen in love with it and spent two years building a house there before announcing to their children that they were leaving them.

Fred was now the dispatcher for the White Pass Railway which transported 100,000 tourists every summer over the old gold rush route to Dawson City. While Eva was like a cloud on legs, Fred's face had been hacked out of granite, and he went at conversations in the same way.

Luther, meanwhile, was from Tennessee via North Carolina, and took so long finishing his sentences that you almost fell into the soup waiting for the full stop.

The conversation between them was like one of those highly stylised Indian paintings of the 19th
Century in which an elephant proceeds magnificently through the jungle as a tiger snaps at its heels.

"Sharpest grade in North America — three point five," snarled Fred pleasantly at one stage.

"Hayull, nuo, theyus one in Nawth Cyarolinah eyas fawwwwww poyen faiv," said Luther between the soup and the chicken.

I finally left them arguing about the gauge of New Zealand Railways, and ended up in the rear observation car, which was filled with old-timers lit in a ghastly manner from below by the safety light.

After a while I began to feel that it was only a matter of time before we crossed the River Styx, a suspicion confirmed when the conductor called up from the bar: "Final call, folks."

It was the last straw.

I returned to my bedroom, only to receive a further shock. It had been ransacked! Then I realised that was the way I had left it.

Twenty-three

A hundred years ago, Winnipeg was famous only for the width of its streets and the thickness of its mud. It is little changed today.

This morning I wandered down Main Street past the peeling Winnipeg Hotel, whose main attractions, according to the sign outside, were ice-cold beer and weekly rates.

At the end of the next block, beyond the Times Change Blues Club (home of Big Dave McLean and the Buddy-Tones) was the junction of Portage Avenue and Main Street.

With eight lanes, Main is the widest street in Canada because the Red River ox carts used to squeak down it 12 abreast in the 1880s, and Portage, which isn't much narrower, was the trail the buffalo took when they went down to the river to drink. Two thirds of the people I'd met in Canada claimed that this junction was the coldest, wettest, windiest corner in the country.

However, the rest insisted that studies by a group of University of Winnipeg students had proved that it was the corner of Memorial and Broadway, 10 blocks west.

I can now report that the majority has it, by a cold nose.

Underneath the junction was a sprawling new complex of banks, shops and offices, where whey-faced people sat looking miserable, as if they had been locked out of one of the few memorable things that Winnipeg possessed, and denied the daily opportunity to compare temperatures on the famous corner above their heads with that even more famous Canadian expression: "Cold enough for you, eh?"

Less famous, but warmer, was Birt's Saddlery down the street, an airy emporium in which horseless cowboys tried on tooled boots, silver-tipped shirts, rawhide gloves and real Stetsons. I bought a tin sheriff's badge for my Dad to wear when he was watching his favourite John Wayne movies, and found myself shortly after in the Winnipeg Fur Exchange over on Ross Avenue.

Inside, from a wall hung with bear, buffalo, otter, muskrat, wolf, beaver, fox, sheep, rabbit and ox, the front end of a disgruntled moose looked down. Heaven knows where the other end of him was, but it wasn't where it belonged. I left, resisting the temptation to buy a Davy Crockett coonskin hat, and walked back to catch the train.

The streets seemed to be filled with chain-smoking women in cheap dresses and training shoes, tired men in exhausted suits and indolent youths in leather jackets and straining jeans.

Ten minutes later, The Canadian headed west, and I was glad to be on it. Winnipeg had not been uplifting for the soul.

Twenty-four

Herbert was in the lounge reading an article in the Reader's Digest entitled: "Aids — what you should know."

He was 87.

"Can't be too careful," he said in response to the question I hadn't asked him.

Herbert was a retired carpenter from the state of New Hampshire, and had been travelling for so long he'd forgotten when he started.

"You're a bit young to have travelled on these trains in the old days, aren't you? Well, don't believe what anyone tells you — this is a whole lot better," he said.

"In the old days the water was freezing, and the only way you could get a shower was to persuade the conductor to persuade the engineer to stop at a hotel. You went upstairs, had your shower and paid the hotel for it.

"The cook on this train then was a young feller who worked at the Maritime University of Maine in the winters and on the trains in the summers.

"I can't even remember his name. I oughta, because after that I met him working on one of the old windjammer cruises out of Maine.

"He got up at four every morning and cooked bacon and eggs for 30 on a single wood stove. And if you didn't like bacon and eggs, it was just your tough luck.

"But that's just what he was like. One Saturday he was making custard pie and the captain says: 'We're ready to go' and he says: 'Oh no we're not -   we can't leave until the custard sets.'

"So we all had to sit there and wait 20 minutes until the custard pie was ready, and then we sailed.
It was the only ship I ever saw where the cook was over the captain. Course we were all young fellers then, and enjoyed that sort of thing."

He leaned a little closer.

"Say," he said, "do you think we'll see any deer today? I saw six yesterday, but I ain't seen a one today."

So we sat, Herbert and I, looking out of the window for deer. It was almost nightfall, and a hooked moon was rising high above the prairies.

But all we saw, in that great lonely sea of grass, was a tiny graveyard, far from anywhere, marked by a single iron arch.

And all we heard, when the train stopped for one of its many unexplained halts, was the whispering of the grass and the high threnody of the wind in the telegraph wires, like the prayers and hymns of these lonely dead in the faraway languages of Ukraine, Sweden, Finland and Iceland.

And above it all, in the moment before we started, the sound which brought them here, that siren song which is more than anything the national anthem of Canada. The long, lonesome whistle of a train, heading west.

Twenty-five

Lou Hannah was five feet tall, of ancient but uncertain vintage, and talked like a hailstorm on a flat tin roof.

Lou was one of the guides at Boomtown 1910, a reconstruction of a prairies main street in Saskatoon, Saskatchewan. Saskawhere? Saskatoon, I said.

The city was founded in 1882 by a Toronto temperance society, which got hold of even-numbered lots along the Saskatchewan River and offered to sell them for $320 each to settlers who would promise to forsake the demon drink.

The settlers, after sober reflection, bought the odd lots from the Government at $10 each instead.

The town was named after the dry, elegant berries of the area, and the thoroughfares were planned by Charles Powell, who with incurable romanticism called them First Street, Second Avenue and so forth.

Today the descendants of the temperance settlers still live across the river, emerging occasionally in the summer to admire the pelicans or telephone across to complain about the rock concerts in the gardens of the Bessborough Hotel, a mad château of a place built by the Canadian Pacific Railway in the days when architects were real men.

Not to mention newsboys — there's still a bronze statue on the Saskatoon street corner where 15-year-old paper seller John G Diefenbaker met Canadian Prime Minister Sir Wilfred Laurier.

As Laurier tells it: "He talked to me for half an hour, then said: 'Well, Mr Prime Minister, I can't waste any more time; I have to deliver my papers.'"

The newsboy, of course, became PM himself, from 1957 to 1963, and at the Diefenbaker Museum on the university campus, you can pick up a telephone and eavesdrop on the Yukon to Washington call he made to John F Kennedy when the Alaska-Canada phone line was opened in 1962.

Diefenbaker spent most of the conversation complaining to Kennedy for not being there. You almost feel like shouting down the line: "Hey Dief, give Jack a break. He hasn't got much longer, you know!"

Other highlight of the city include Wanuskewin, where you can follow old Indian trails and see how the buffalo were hunted; the Ukrainian Museum, which has a beautiful collection of painted eggshells and vintage embroidery; and the Meewasin pioneer centre on the riverbank, where you can almost see the shock of the faces of the settlers who, tempted to Canada by imaginative advertising campaigns featuring bustling farms and hustling cities, arrived to find only the rustling wilderness.

Still, even they knew more about Canada than the party of VIPs from the Vietnamese Ministry of Travel who were being shown around Meewasin in the morning I was there. "Alberta is on one side, and Manitoba is on the other," the interpreter was patiently explaining.

And then there was Lou, who was brought up in little Kenaston and moved to Saskatoon in 1942, where she reached the giddy domestic heights of having an ice box which the wagon refilled twice a week.

"They always came after I'd waxed the floor, sir. Humph," she said outside the barber's, followed closely by: "That lampshade over there is Tiffany — that's a name for good stuff in a jewellery shop."

We stopped briefly beside a threshing machine from Stevens Turner of London, Ontario, and I foolishly asked her why the Ns were all back to front.

"People out east didn't know any better," she said without pausing in an arthritic sprint to the City Garage.

"This is a 1912 Hupmobile but I don't know much about it I don't drive never have sir," she
announced.

I was about to lend her a few commas I had to spare, but she was already outside the millinery shop.

"See those buttonhole shoes? My brother sold gopher tails to buy me a pair just like them. But every morning I howled because I never could find the buttonholer, and I didn't ever get another pair, sir.

"See those bathing suits? Men wore cotton ones, so when they got wet they left nothing to the imagination, as you can imagine, sir. Just stuck right through them, you didn't know where to look.

"The women wore woollen, but my sister wrapped a blanket around her down to the edge of the water, even in front of the family.

"And this here's the Wing Lee Chinese Laundry, started by the boys who worked on the railway.

"See that, sir? That's a special wimple crimper for an order of nuns whose wimple pleats ran vertically. It would have been heated by coals placed inside.

"And that's a gasoline iron. I had one when they came out, but I only used it when my husband
Dalton was home, in case I got blown to Kingdom Come and he didn't.

"See those artificial horses beside the blacksmith's, sir? Dalton made those. The mane and tails are real — one Saturday he was eating his supper and he heard there was a horse killed over by the railway tracks, and he jumped up and ran off to get the hair for these.

"When his friends called for him, I told them he was out chasing a dead horse before I realised what
I was saying."

By the time we reached the general hardware store, Lou had woven her spell so convincingly that I wanted to live in Main Street, Canada in 1910, sitting down for a game of checkers by the counter while my wife splashed out on the latest candle maker, bottle capper, corn sheller and stocking stretcher.

There was only one problem. I would never earn enough to pay for all that stuff working as a stoker for a coal-fired vertical wimple crimper.

Twenty-six

To say that Serge Pigeon was dapper is like describing Moby Dick as a fishing yarn.

From the top of his regulation felt hat down to riding boots sparkling with 50 layers of polish, wax and spit, Serge was every inch a Royal Canadian Mounted Policeman.

And so he should be - he'd just spent six months graduating from the RCMP Academy in Regina, Saskatchewan.

Regina, a bright, friendly city filled on this fresh spring day with the buzz of saws and tap of hammers, was originally called Pile O'Bones because of the enormous heap of buffalo skeletons left there by native kills. In 1882 it was renamed Regina after Queen Victoria, much to the scorn of the citizens, but that same year it was also selected as the home of the Mounties, which is why millions of visitors flock there today.

Getting there as a tourist is certainly the easiest way in — before the force accepted Serge, they spent a year and a half not only interviewing and testing him, but talking to his friends, family and neighbours.

After that it was up at 5.30 every morning to iron the sheets and make the bed, then out for a day of study, self-defence, driving, firearms and drill. Swimming was the best part, except for those who couldn't. They were ordered to dive in at the deep end.

After that, showing tourists around the academy was a bit of a doodle.

"Although I do feel sorry when I see a new troop starting out. They just don't know what's ahead of them," said Serge, standing in the drill hall.

Behind him, drill instructor Corporal Ian Ferguson was politely enquiring: "Is there any obvious reason why you're doing push-ups with your arse in the air, Doyle?"

"No, Corporal," muttered the unfortunate Doyle.

After Doyle had been suitably dealt with, it was time for lunch, at which hundreds of earnest young men and women sat around munching beef and potatoes and keeping their eyes open for criminals, and then the daily drill call, when the two best troops parade under the flag of the province and the twin withering gazes of Sgt Major Sandy Mahon and a dead buffalo on the wall.

One recruit was wearing black boots because his brown ones were being repaired, two were in navy jackets because the brown ones had worn out, and five were in choir practice.

But then, the motto of Saskatchewan is From Many People Strength, and one day from many jackets, boots and choirboys would emerge Mounties.

Lunch finished, the resident band played Waltzing Matilda, and they all went marching off to get their man.

One day, Serge and Sam Steele would be proud of them. Col Steele was one of the first members of the original Mounties sent out to keep the peace in the West. In a time of heroes, he was the most heroic of them all, and the Maxim machineguns with which he and his men guarded White Pass during the Klondike gold rush can still be seen in the museum at Regina today.

Beside the museum stands the little wooden chapel which is the oldest building in Regina. In former days, members of the force were not allowed to marry for five years, but today, the chapel is where many Mounties get their woman.

Outside the Mountie Academy, where the highlight during the summer is the daily sunset ceremony, there is much to see in Regina, including the beautiful 2300-acre Wascana Park, where the lakes were dug out by unemployed men in the depression of the Thirties. Wascana is where Regina goes walking, canoeing across to Willow Island for picnics, or sleigh riding in winter.

Another must is the restored interior of Government House, where, standing in the drawing room, the guide informed me with perfect innocence: "Before the ballroom was built, the Lieutenant Governor held his balls in here."

The natural history and science museums are also excellent, with the latter including a huge Imax cinema. At the science museum, children can make bubbles, test their strength, see what their voice sounds like and make their hair stand on end, and adults can look guilty when caught enjoying themselves.

Later that day, with my hair still refusing to sit down, I ate at the Copper Kettle, a greasy spoon joint near the hotel. The only other occupant was the noisiest eater in Regina. He kept up a constant drumbeat of knife and plate with one hand and stirred his coffee to death with the other, then slurped it all the way through his bacon and eggs before concluding with a fair rendition of the Trumpet Voluntary through his napkin.

I had chicken, gave a couple of dollars outside to a native with a sob story about a wrecked car, and walked to the bus station, leaving behind only a pile of bones on a plate.

As my mother said, you should always leave things as you found them.

Twenty-seven

There are only two potential disasters on an overnight bus journey: the fat person beside you and the crying child in front.

I got both. Fortunately, this being Canada, the child was a little angel, and the fat woman offered to change places so I could have more legroom.

Unfortunately, there then emerged a third challenger — the man with the hacking cough.

It was his fault that I slept so fitfully on the first night of my journey north from Edmonton to the Yukon. The only thing that stopped me from committing very justifiable homicide was the thought that I was having it much easier than the pioneers, canoeing across lakes and up rivers, then portaging their way across land. You had to be careful not to mix the two up, or you ended up swimming across icy lakes with a canoe on your head, and paddling like mad through the forest.

Dawn rose fretfully to reveal snowy hills cloaked by forests, and as we drew near to Dawson Creek I could tell that we were entering a land where the way of life had been pared down to the basics. It was the log cabins in the trees, with their breakfast smoke curling up into the still, cold air. It was the horses in the corral. It was the McDonald's sign down the road.

Dawson Creek, the end of the first night of the journey, was mile zero on the Canada-Alaska Highway, built by US troops in 1942 as a military road and later upgraded for civilian use. The 1,520 miles was finished by 19,000 men and 11,000 machines in eight months, including one of the worst winters on record.

Today it is one of the world's great drives, and this year celebrations all along the route will mark its 50th anniversary. For the sleepy villages along the route, like Dawson Creek and Whitehorse, the highway meant the end of isolation forever.

But in Dawson Creek, some things hadn't changed all that much in 50 years. In the bus terminal, the two magazines available were Prairie Overcomer (Today's Religious Magazine for Victorious Living) and Bingo News & Gaming Hi-Lites (Spotlight on Blind Curling Inside).

The Editor's Comments section of Bingo News read: "Easter break is upon is, as I well know; my telephone has been ringing fairly consistently with a little voice on the line asking: 'Granny, how many more days 'til I come stay at your house?'

"The celebration of Christ's death and resurrection is important to myself and my family. We colour eggs, eat a lot, visit, share, love and worship together."

From outside came the cry of the driver: "All aboard for the north."

I shouldered my pack and stepped into the frozen morning, leaving Dawson Creek secure in the knowledge that the Lord was going to have a full house at Easter.

Twenty-eight

The good news, as the bus headed north from Dawson Creek, was that the fat woman sitting beside me and the potentially crying child in front had both disembarked.

The bad news was that the man with the hacking cough was with us all the way to Whitehorse in the Yukon, 18 hours away.

Any initial sympathy anyone had felt for him had been swept away the moment he leaped off the bus at the first stop and began smoking three cigarettes at once. By now, the general feeling on the bus was that lynching him would be a waste of a good rope.

And things were getting worse. Between coughs, he was busy having conversations with his grandmother which made Sylvester Stallone sound like Albert Einstein.

''Like some chocolate, grandmaw? I think I'll have some. Cough! Cough! Or a Crunchie bar. I like Crunchie bars, always have. Cough! Cough!"

I was going to go mad. Cough! Cough! No, I had to relax. Cough! Cough! Travelling was about journeys more than arrivals, and flying was for wimps. Wasn't it? Cough! Cough!

At Pink Mountain, so called because it was covered in white snow and green trees, we stopped for breakfast. Everyone else on the bus traipsed into the Pink Mountain Restaurant for coffee, hash browns, bacon and eggs.

But I needed a cough break more than hot food. I walked across the highway to the General Store.

"No 'dogs' allowed. No shoes, No shirt, No service," said the sign on the door.

The proprietress leaped out from behind a television and stood expectantly behind the counter as I opened the door of an ancient fridge. Inside was a bottle of lemonade, a block of cheese, two ham rolls and a can of Kokanee beer (Brewed Right Here in the Kootenays).

I bought the lot, and returned to aural martyrdom on the bus. Cough! Cough! At Prophet River, a little girl in bright clothes was playing on a tyre swing in front of a half-built log cabin, her golden Labrador's head swaying as he watched her swing in the sun on the edge of the forest.

As we trundled north, the evergreens gave way now and then to ghostly copses of silver birch. Above our heads, their soft branches brushed the northern sky a paler blue. And beside us, the man with the cough began telling his grandmother that he was convinced he had extra-sensory perception.

"Remember when Uncle Bawb died? I knew that was going to happen. Cough! Cough!"

Grandmaw looked up at the sky, and wished she was with Uncle Bawb.

We crawled on, past rivers where the spring ice creaked and groaned and along the feet of mountains where great slides of snow hung perilously. We were silent, fearful that the man with the cough would bring an avalanche crashing down upon us.

Now and then, shacks and motels emerged out of the forest, beckoning the traveller in to no comforts other than warmth and food. We stopped at one, the Wilderness Restaurant and Motel beside frozen Muncho Lake, and the driver got off, to deliver a single fresh lettuce.

And then, as darkness fell, we drew up at Laird River Lodge.

Above the door in the gathering gloom, there was a carved leprechaun. Inquiries with the owners revealed that the lodge had been built by Irishman Tim O'Rourke and his wife years before.

But why the O'Rourkes had come to the end of the earth and opened this lonely roadhouse, and where they had gone since, remained a mystery as we drove away into the setting sun, passing on the way the hot springs where you can swim on a winter evening and watch as the moose come silently down through the forest to stand there among the trees, their nostrils steaming and their lost, innocent eyes watching you as darkness falls.

In that darkness, somewhere between sleep and awakening, and in a silence mysteriously unbroken by a single cough, we passed into the Yukon.

Twenty-nine

In the bright spring sunshine today, with a fresh breeze blowing in from the ocean, the main street of Skagway in Alaska could almost be mistaken for heaven on earth. But in the autumn of 1897, it was the gateway to hell.

For most of the gold stampeders lured north by the headlines shouting: "Gold!" in the popular newspapers of William Randolph Hearst, Skagway was the first landfall after the ferry north from Seattle.

Here they poured in their tens of thousands, paddling ashore in the bay through horses, goats, mules and oxen dumped off the ferries and left to swim ashore. Here they dumped their supplies on the mudflats, often returning to find them ruined by the tide and their journey over.

And down this main street called Broadway they poured. Here, if they wished, they could eat salmon stewed in champagne at the Pack Trail restaurant and buy a woman for the night in Paradise Alley while the streets echoed with shooting and the screams of those dying from meningitis or a thousand other plagues.

And here, if they were unlucky, they ran into 'Reverend' Charles Bowers, Slim Jim Foster or Old Man Tripp, three of the smooth-talking con men in the gang of Randolph 'Soapy' Smith, the self-styled dictator of Skagway who made a fortune relieving stampeders of their grubstake.

For Skagway was in US territory, and the closest law and order was Colonel Sam Steele and his Mounties, up there on the peak of White Pass on the brand new Canadian border.

Smith's reign finally ended in the summer of 1898 in a shootout with surveyor Frank Reid, who died 12 days later of his injuries.

Both are buried in the little graveyard on a rise among the trees, just out of town down the railroad tracks. A bunch of fresh carnations lay on Reid's grave today, below the inscription: "He gave his life for the honor of Skagway."

Nearby is the grave of Ella Wilson, an 18-year-old prostitute who plied her trade in Paradise Alley and died in 1898. The citizens of Skagway, with the wry sense of humour needed to live in such a place, inscribed her headstone: "She gave her honor for the life of Skagway."

But the most fascinating grave of all is that of the man who walked into the Canadian Bank of Commerce at 3pm on September 15, 1902, with several sticks of dynamite and a pistol under his coat. As he attempted to pull his pistol out, it went off, discharging the dynamite. Only his head was found, and the good citizens dutifully bore it to the graveyard and buried it under a wooden slab on which they painted the single word: "Unknown".

And so they lie here among the trees, the heroes and villains, the winners and losers of Skagway, looking down the railroad tracks to the town where they lived and died.

In the distance, you can just see the site of Dyea, which in 1897 had a population of 10,000, 48 hotels, 47 restaurants and 39 taverns. Two years later, every building had been torn down and shipped elsewhere, and today there is nothing, except the wind in the trees and the little track which leads to the start of the Chilkoot Trail over the mountains.

The 30,000 stampeders who set out here were glad to leave the hell of Skagway behind. Little did they know that compared to what lay ahead, they had just turned their backs on paradise.

And so did I, driving away in a hire car past a row of iron ore trucks heading for the nearest orehouse as behind me the hot afternoon sun turned the snowy mountains into something disturbingly familiar.

It was half an hour before I realised what it was. Baked Alaska, funnily enough.

Thirty

When the stampeders set off from Skagway in the summer of 1897 they would take the best part of a year to reach Dawson City on the Klondike River, 600 miles away.

It took me nine hours by car.

For those on foot, the long trail north began with a 33-mile trek over the Chilkoot Pass to Lake Bennett.

Because the Mounties would not let any of them in with less than a year's supply of food, each stampeder had to trek back and forward up to 40 times before he was done.

Many died of cold or malnutrition, or went mad and killed themselves. By the time the survivors reached Bennett, stinking, exhausted and sick with dysentery, the 33 miles had taken most of them three months.

Those who could afford a horse took the White Pass trail instead, overloading and beating their animals in their frantic desire for gold. Over 3,000 horses died on White Pass and were left to rot. Those which fell on the trail were literally trampled into the ground, their head and tail sticking out of the ground on either side. One man lit a fire under his exhausted oxen and watched as they were roasted alive, unable to move.

It is hard to believe today that such things happened, driving up from Skagway between snowy mountains which the restless sun drapes and redrapes constantly with veils of shade, and past Emerald Lake, the most aptly named stretch of water in the world.

At Bennett Lake, the stampeders built rafts and crossed to Carcross, where they spent the winter waiting for the thaw so that they could build or buy boats for the remaining 560 miles past Whitehorse to Dawson City.

Whitehorse today is the home of the MacBride Museum, where the characters of those days, too numerous to list, gaze out from photographs on the wall. The capital of the Yukon, it is also the staging post for another form of stampede today, of the 225,000 tourists who flock to the territory every year, including an increasing number of Japanese.

Since Oriental legend has it that a child conceived under the northern lights will be male, the only
sound on the twilight streets of Whitehorse in the summer is the discreet squeak of bedsprings as pairs of Japanese tourists lovingly turn the Yukon into the land of the midnight son.

From Whitehorse, the road winds steadily north, through sandy deserts which were the bottom of inland seas and past vast glittering lakes which no one has bothered to name. And very, very occasionally, high on an icy hill, there is the log cabin of a soul who, like many in the Yukon, came here for two weeks 20 years ago and fell in love with this infinity of solitude.

I stopped for a picnic at Rock Lake, where the previous diners had overturned the rubbish barrel. I was about to tidy it up when I noticed that their footprints were those of bears.

I left, quite quickly. Ahead of me, the road stretched into a vast and wonderful wilderness. Every so often, out of the shining forests of birch would emerge a log cabin with a rough-hewn sign outside offering warmth and food.

But I would never find out what the homemade soup at Moose Lodge or the soft beds at Partridge Creek Farm were like, for they would not be open for another month, and I would be long gone by then.

Finally, as night grew near, I found Dawson, a motley panjandrum of bright clapboard buildings hiding behind several piles of snow.

I booked into the Eldorado Hotel and ordered roast pork. They brought me half a pig, washed down with a bottle of wine. It cost me $22.

In 1898 in Dawson, that amount wouldn't even have bought me the wine, at a time when the average wage elsewhere was a dollar a day.

After dinner, I searched the snow-covered streets. But there was no sign of a McDonald's.

Truly, I had reached the end of the trail.

So when I sat down to dinner in the hotel that evening, I asked the waitress, a small girl with a big smile and a waterfall of dark hair pinned up in a tottering chignon.

"Got anything local?" I said.

"Red snapper. Caught in that river over there," she said, tilting her head towards the window.

"What, no freshly killed moose smothered in maple syrup? No grizzly soufflé?"

She shook her head, sending several pins tinkling to the wooden floor.

But a minute later she was back. The red snapper was off. So was the roast duck, the pork and the snails.

"So have you got any local specialities?" I said.

She thought for a moment.

"Fettucine?" she said.

Thirty-one

It is a sunny afternoon in August 1896, and you are drifting in the riverboat of your imagination down Rabbit Creek towards the Klondike River in the Yukon, your senses brimming with the scent of wild rose and raspberry.

Suddenly, as you round a bend, the air is split with wild cries, and you see three men dancing and shouting at the top of their voices. Slowly, the scene fades away.

Now it is a bright April morning in 1992, and you are standing in the middle of a dirt street in
Dawson, just down the river from that scene you witnessed almost a hundred years ago. In front of the Westminster Hotel, two men are wrestling in the mud, watched with interest by an enormous raven and a single husky lying in the middle of the street.

In front of you is standing Buffalo Taylor, the world's greatest living expert on Dawson. Even in a town where everyone holds down at least three jobs, Buffalo is Renaissance man writ large. He is, at various times, assistant deputy fire chief, director of the Klondike Visitors' Association, vice president of the Chamber of Commerce, chairman and proprietor of the firefighters' museum, president of the Dempster Highway Bus Service, boss of Gold City Tours, local agent for Air North and Alcan, proprietor of Dawson Limousines and owner of Flora Dora's Hotel.

Even his friends cannot agree why exactly he is called Buffalo. Some say it is because he is built like one, while others insist equally fervently that it is because his moustache bears a remarkable resemblance to a fine pair of horns. But then Dawson's like that. You hear four different versions of every legend, each one the sworn truth, and each one as entertaining as the next.

The good citizens, undeterred by the fact that many of the Gold Rush buildings burnt down several times over, have simply built them again with the same gaudy frontier spirit that made Dawson swell from a swamp to a city of 30,000 in two years.

And what a city it was, where men dug fortunes out of the dirt and tumbled into town with the dirt still on them to spend $3,000 buying drinks for all in a single mad night, where the can-can girls danced all week and bathed in wine bought by admirers, but men were fined by the Mounties for using vile language on the Sabbath.

A city where men like Harry Woolrich won $60,000 one night, decided to quit gambling, then lost it the next day while waiting for the ferry out, or men like Harry Kimbal, who spent $300,000 in a three-month binge.

Today, with a permanent population of fewer than 1,000, Dawson is the only city in the world where the local tourist officials happily admit to being corrupt — they get their budget from the profits of Diamond Tooth Gertie's Casino -where you can still drink hard liquor, watch soft girls dancing the can-can, and lose your paydirt at blackjack, red dog and Texas hold'em.

Gertie's, named after the dance hall queen who wore a diamond between her two front teeth, is one of an increasing number of buildings restored to their gold rush liveliness in Dawson.

Others include the Palace Grand Theatre, built in 1899 by Arizona Charlie Meadows, who appeared on stage nightly to shoot an egg from the hand of his wife May — until the night he shot off her thumb. For only $13.50, you can hire a box at the Palace and sit where the dance hall girls used to entice the miners up, to buy them drink at $50 a bottle, which they then poured into a drain on the floor to be rebottled and sold again.

Also being restored, although not to full working order, is Ruby Scott's, the last brothel in the Yukon, where right up to the Sixties miners would still pay social calls on Ruby's 'nieces'.

The city museum will also seduce you back to the boom and bust days with a two-room display. The reason it's so small is because the whole city is a museum, filled with characters like Two by Four Bob, who got his nickname from felling a fellow miner with a length of the same over a disputed claim. He would have got away with it except for the 200 witnesses.

Or Art Fry, former boxing champion of the Yukon. Or the NASA scientist who gave it all up to earn $100 a month mining the creeks by hand.

Walking through the streets, you're never quite sure which century you're in, as you watch miners going into the post office to register a claim, or stand before the shack in which Jack London wrote White Fang and Call of the Wild, or walk past the cabin where Robert Service penned ballads like The Shooting of Dan McGrew and The Cremation of Sam McGee after his day's work at the Bank of Commerce along the street. Just down the hill is the wooden home of Pierre Berton, the Canadian writer whose book Klondike is compulsory reading for anyone on the gold rush trail.

And then, down the road out of town and right at the sign marked Bonanza, the real story begins. As Buffalo and I bumped in his truck along the frozen track beside what was once called Rabbit Creek, he was discoursing knowledgeably on hydraulics and permafrost and bedrock, but I'm afraid I wasn't listening.

I was looking at the side of the track, counting off the magical numbers painted in white on the bottom of rusty buckets sticking out of the snow: BD16, BD15, BD14, with every bucket taking us 500ft closer to the Eden of Capitalism, to the claim they called Discovery.

Today, only a simple cairn marks the spot where on that hot August afternoon in 1896 you saw George Washington Carmack, Skookum Jim and Tagish Charlie dancing a jig of joy after they found a nugget the size of a thumb. The legends about who actually found it are legion.

The most common is that Jim was washing up in the stream when he found the nugget in a dish, woke up the sleeping Carmack and said: "Is this what you're looking for?"

Carmack left the other two to guard the site and rushed down to the town of Fortymile to register the claim.

He told everyone he met on the way. Some dropped everything and raced to the scene, but others ignored 'Lying George' and went on their way, a fortune slipping from their grasp. Within days, Fortymile was a ghost town and all of Rabbit Creek had been staked and renamed Bonanza. Past there is Eldorado Creek, which was even richer.

After government surveyor William Ogilvie redrew some of the claims later that year, he revealed a pie-shaped section of unclaimed ground on Eldorado 86ft at its widest point. Prospector Dick Lowe asked Ogilvie if he wanted it, but the incorruptible surveyor said he would not, since he was a government official. Lowe claimed the site, then changed his mind and tried to sell it, but there were no takers because it was so small. Lowe's Fraction, as it became known, made him $500,000. He squandered the lot.

Others became rich by accident. Charley Anderson woke up one morning to find that he had bought an untested Eldorado claim for $800 while he was drunk the night before. When the police told him he couldn't get his $800 back, he started digging. The claim was worth $1,000,000, and for the rest of his life, Anderson was known as The Lucky Swede.

Further down the creek is the 3,000-tonne dredger built by another of Dawson's legends, Joe Boyle, in 1913. Three years later, Boyle raised a volunteer machine gun battalion from the men of the city and went off to fight in the war in Europe. Decorated by both the Romanian and Russian governments after rescuing the Romanian royal family, he died in England in 1923. The dredgers of Boyle and others have worked Bonanza and Eldorado over the years, taking at least $500 million out of them.

But there are still men there, who cling to the dream of another time. One of them is Henry Rennink, a former logger from Ontario, who has spent the last eight years on Eldorado in temperatures hitting 60 below. As Buffalo and I walked up the frozen creek, he was winching a bucket up from the 43ft shaft he had spent all winter digging by hand, thawing the ground with steam from a home-made boiler. He came walking down the slope towards us with the nervous, excited air of a man who was just about to become rich, tomorrow or the day after.

"Here, let me show you a couple of nuggets, eh?" he said, running into his shack and emerging with the little cotton bag which miners used to empty on the bar with a cry of: "Set her up, boys; the drinks are on me!", and which they still call their poke.

Henry placed on the palm of my hand a lump of gleaming metal worth $7,000. So this was it. My heart began to beat faster, and in that second I was back on that sunny August afternoon in 1896.

Except I was one of the ones on the bank, dancing and shouting the same word, over and over again: "Gold!"

Thirty-two

Even in a country where coincidence had become an art form, I blinked.

But it was still there. The advertisement on Dawson City TV definitely said: "Every Sunday on Radio CFYT, Rock the Klondike from 3 to 5 with DJ Sean Fenn, the Belfast Kid."

He couldn't be. Could he?

He was. The man who was shipping rock into a town famous for shipping rocks out was from dear old Ulster.

As I found out when I met him later, Sean, aka Joe Magee, was born in Ballyhackamore in east Belfast 36 years ago and emigrated to Canada in 1974.

"I had a sister and brother-in-law in Calgary, so I moved there and did a one-year course in broadcasting," said Joe, sipping a Molson in the bar of the Eldorado Hotel in Dawson.

"Then I moved into auto parts and couriering, working part time as a DJ, but in the last couple of years I got a bit sick and tired of the city, and some friends in Dawson said that I couldn't get much further from a city than here."

Sean, his German-born wife Andrea, and their sons Russell, three, and four-month-old Derek, arrived in Dawson in March.

"It was 40 below the day we got here, and I thought: 'My God, what have I let myself in for?' but then four days later I got chatting to the head of the local radio station, and he offered me work as a DJ on the Sunday show," he said.

In an area where the hills usually echoed to the winsome strains of country music, Joe's diet of Queen, Supertramp and Genesis was an instant hit.

"There seem to be a lot of old hippies in Dawson who love Sixties and Seventies stuff. They all phoned the radio station the next day and said: 'Hey, dudes, it's great to hear some real music on the station instead of that country and western crap'."

In fact, he was such a hit that he was just about to become the Yukon's latest TV superstar, introducing the Thursday video show. And if that comes off, he and the family are planning a rare visit home.

"I was back last Christmas for only the second time in 17 years, and I couldn't believe how clean and busy Belfast was. It was like a little New York.

"And my own area's changed beyond recognition. All the pubs and bookies have become pharmacists and estate agents.

"But I like Dawson. You can be whatever you like here. We'll be here for at least a couple of years, I reckon," he said, looking out of the bar window as one of the enormous ravens which haunts the town sailed over half a dozen huskies padding aimlessly up the dirt street.

They were scattered by Buffalo Taylor in his role as deputy assistant fire chief and proprietor of Dawson's firefighters' museum, racing past on his way to inspect a 1900 Aherne steamer he'd got wind of up by Moose Creek.

Ahead of The Belfast Kid stretched 24 months of homespun highlights like the sweepstake to guess when the river ice breaks up, and the Great Klondike Outhouse Race, when teams race around the town pulling someone sitting on an outside toilet. And the Klondike Sun, the monthly newspaper which had that day exclusively reported a sighting of Princess Diana driving a bulldozer up by the creeks.

The Belfast Kid and his family would be toasted in the summer, and frozen in the winter.

But as I left Dawson the next morning, I could see what had drawn him there.

Everyone I had met in the Yukon had assured me that I would be back to this infinity of solitude, with its distant mountains, its great rivers crackling with ice and its log cabins with woodsmoke curling blue against the forest and a warm welcome inside. That I would be back, drawn by the call of the wild as men had been drawn here a hundred years ago by the lure of gold.

I was thinking all this as I drove away, and then I sneezed.

Cold! I had caught cold in the Yukon.

What a strange thing fate is, I thought, as Dawson City disappeared around the bend in my rear-view mirror.

But for a single letter, I would have been a rich man.

Thirty-three

Dawn in the mountains of northern British Columbia brought a scene of almost indescribable beauty, as I returned south on the bus from the Yukon to Edmonton.

There had been a heavy snowfall overnight, and below me coils of mist boiled in the hollows of the forest as the sun rose a bloody orange, bathing the crystal scene in countless fiery hues.

I hunted out my camera, waited for the moment when the scene before me would have made the most jaded cynic weep with tears of joy, and pressed the button.

Nothing happened.

I had forgotten to wind on, and in the next moment we sank into the seething cauldron of white. I
looked around, feeling nervously sheepish, but none of the other four occupants of the Greyhound had noticed.

There was Dwayne over there, wearing his tie-dyed T-shirt, reading Douglas Adams and munching one of the carrots which were all he ate. Every so often, he would put down the book and scribble frantically in a notebook.

When he went to the toilet, I grabbed a look at what he was writing.

"Yggdrasil," it said at the top of the page. And then: "It was the 364th summer that J D Orcwing had spent on Greylag, named after some long-dead bird on a planet he'd never heard of, and he was getting a little sick and tired of the place ... "

Dwayne returned from his ablutions, picked up his biro, and returned to the great work. But after a few minutes, he returned to munching his carrot and gazing out of the window.

Far away, on a planet Dwayne had never heard of, Douglas Adams breathed a sigh of relief.

Then there was Cynthia, a very enormous Tlingit Indian who wore neon clothes and had so many coughing fits that they threatened to turn into coffin fits. Perhaps she was a distant cousin of the man who had driven an entire busload of people mad with his coughing on my way north a week ago.

And then there was Janeece, a flawless beauty therapist from Calgary who had been up to visit Mick, her mechanic husband who had secured a lucrative post in the one-moose hamlet of Watson Lake. Janeece had pronounced herself satisfied with Watson Lake and was now heading south, draped in a pink coverlet and reading Barbara Cartland, to pack her nail file and rejoin Mick.

It was wonderful to think of. He would head out into the blizzards every morning with his nails immaculate and come home every evening to a warm cucumber face pack.

And finally there was Jeff, a small wiry man with a face halfway between drowned rat and eager puppy. He had been travelling ever since his wife died, and was heading home to New Brunswick to build houses. He delighted in telling everyone he met how he had spent two days trying to hitch out of Watson Lake before giving up and catching the bus.

"Two days, eh?" he chuckled to himself. "Different story in Whitehorse: hardly had time to put my bag down before somebody stopped. Not too friendly, these Watson Lake folk, eh, Janeece?"

Janeece smiled and returned to page 138, where Grant, his eyes smouldering and his manhood well ablaze, was ripping the bodice off a trembling Anna with such passion that Janeece bit a flawless fingernail.

"Damn!" she gasped.

"Eh?" said Jeff as Cynthia plunged into another coughing fit and Dwayne absentmindedly picked up his carrot and began writing with it.

Far away, on a planet called Earth, church bells rang out joyously to proclaim that it was the morning of Easter Sunday.

Thirty-four

Jasper is a town of ten million shops, 2,000 people and a totem pole.

There is a little Lutheran church, for little Lutherans, and a herd of elk in the car park every evening.

Held safety in the palm of the Rockies, it is for all the world like a Swiss village with the cuckoo clocks running slow.

In Jasper, the joggers walk, and the favourite occupation of the locals on lazy summer evenings, when they've finished providing the tourists with tasteful souvenirs, is to lie under the pines on the grassy slopes in front of the park ranger's office and watch the mountains go by.

The tourists, meanwhile, have staggered to their rental cars and headed off down to the Icefields Parkway to Banff, a 179-mile drive which must be one of the finest stretches of road God and a steamroller ever put on this earth.

If you do yourself one favour before you die, drive this road.

Wind down the window, breath in the damp piney air, and just stop a minute while that elk crosses to the other side. A couple of miles out of Jasper, turn right, take the Skytram 7,500ft to the top of Whistler Mountain, and have lunch in the clouds.

Then get back into the car and drive on. Soon, you'll realise that you're going slower and slower, because you want this drive to last forever, because you know that you will never see sights like this again. Above your head, the soft underbellies of clouds are torn open by the jagged peaks, and snow comes fluttering down.

Finally you slow to a halt, and turn off the engine. In all the world, the only sound is a starling, deep in the forest, and the nothing sound of snow falling on your upturned face.

The snow becomes rain, and the rain becomes glorious sunshine.

You decide you are so content that you can go no further, and you spend the night in one of the lodges along the way, sleeping in a log cabin under down while outside your window the moon dances in an emerald lake.

Tomorrow you will see another host of wonders, like the Columbia Icefields, a frozen sea which pours through the mountains in a dozen glacial waterfalls.

And Lake Louise, the stretch of water found by Canadian Pacific Rail way surveyor Tom Wilson in 1882. "As God is my judge, I never in all my explorations saw such a matchless scene," said Wilson, who called it Emerald Lake. It was almost immediately given its present name after the fourth daughter of Queen Victoria, neither of whom ever visited it.

It was their loss, but you will find all that out tomorrow when you stop on your way down to Banff, which you will find a little different to the town you left yesterday.

Back in Jasper, the locals leave their Jeeps running while they nip into the post office and the tourists head off into the forest with battered packs slung over their shoulders.

But in Banff, the locals tend to lock up their Mazda convertibles when they head off for a night's jazz at the town theatre, while the tourists emerge from the Banff Springs Hotel to buy a couple of Cartier sweatshirts on their way to the Grizzly House for a reviving plateful of rattlesnake fondue ($55.95 plus tax).

The Banff Springs, probably the best place in the world to spend your honeymoon, is a magnificent baronial pile near the hot springs which gave it its name, and where you can still sit and simmer while the snow hisses into the water around you.

At the Banff Springs, the waiters glide silently to and fro bearing silver trays. In Jasper's equivalent, the Jasper Park Lodge, they arrive at your log cabin on a bicycle.

Both hotels are part of the Canadian Pacific chain, as is the Chateau Lake Louise between the two towns. Lesser mortals stay at places like the Astoria in Jasper or the Banff Park Lodge in Banff.

In Banff, the hotel manager may send up a basket of fruit and a bottle of wine if you're a valued customer. In Jasper, he'll buy you a beer, find out where you can get your favourite Levi's patched (Mrs Potter on Maligne Road will do them for $3, since you ask) and tell you where you can go and jump in a freezing lake watched only by half a dozen curious mountain goats.

Whether you use Jasper or Banff as a base depends on how fresh your credit card is and whether you prefer dead rattlesnake or live elks.

But visit both. Each one is a pearl at the end of the same string, that glittering Icefields Parkway.

Drive it before you die. That way you're sure of heaven.

Thirty-five

The railway between Jasper and Vancouver was the end of the line for many of the men who built it between 1881 and 1882.

If you had stood here in the spring of that first year, you would have seen a miracle taking place as engineers swung off giddy ropes against the dripping faces of the mountains.

Then the drillers would clamber down to cut open the spot which the engineer had marked and fill them with black powder.

As soon as they had scrambled to safety, the blast would gouge out another few stubborn feet of rock. Half a mile west, the men building a wooden trestle bridge hundreds of feet above a raging river wouldn't even raise their heads as the mountains echoed with thunder.

There were other miracles taking place, too, apart from the daily one of forcing a railway through mountains many thought impassable.

In November 1882, a locomotive speeding down a newly-laid section hit a rockslide with such force that it somersaulted over a 250ft embankment and landed upright on a rivcrbank. The fireman and engineer clambered out unhurt.

Others were not so lucky. Men died on this stretch — blown to pieces, toppling off cliff edges, or hurtling uncontrollably down sections of track built steep to save money for the near-bankrupt Canadian Pacific Railway.

Seven thousand of them were Chinese, slaving for half the white man's wage to save the £150 needed to buy a farm in Kwang Tung province at home.

Most of them never made it. After paying for his passage, rent and food, the average coolie was left with £21 for a year of toil.

Ironically, many of the tourists filling the observation dome of The Canadian today were from that endlessly fascinating country off the Chinese coast.

Each of them, of course, would find it just as impossible to return home and buy enough land for a farm as their neighbours did a century ago.

Just before teatime, they erupted into sudden paroxysms of delight. Although my Japanese is rusty, as far as I could make out they were crying: "Oh look, a bear!"

And so it was — a baby grizzly ambling along the edge of the forest.

As he disappeared, the Japanese contingent sank into their seats, the expressions of glee on their faces passing almost simultaneously into ones of horror.

For it had all happened so fast that not one of them had thought of taking a photograph. And
therefore, according to one of the mores of contemporary Japanese mythology, the bear had ceased to exist.

An atmosphere of gloom pervaded the dome and lasted well into the evening, when a moose was spotted sipping the edge of a lake, and his praises sung by a dozen shutters in close harmony.

Peace descended with the evening. In the meandered valleys of the Rockies, cows grazed and women waved from porches as their dogs raced towards pickups rattling home over cattle grids and their children warmed their hands on bonfires.

The cows in the fields shifted nervously as they caught the scent of steaks sizzling on the barbecue. It was Saturday evening, and Canada was eating out.

As darkness fell we entered Kamloops, which in 1884 was a single street of shacks filled with men sleeping on floors and billiard tables while they waited for the railway to arrive.

The circuit judge, George Walkem, was carried to bed dead drunk at 7.30 every morning, and was in court three hours later dispensing heavy fines for drunkenness without batting an eyelid.

Today, most of the 63,000 houses sprawled over the twinkling hillside had satellite dishes outside.

In the early reaches of the night we slid through Yale, a gold rush town after the Cariboo strikes on 1858.

In the streets then, long-haired Indians carrying freshly speared salmon brushed shoulders with
Englishmen in bowler hats, turbaned Hindus and women in the latest Paris fashions.

There were five local Irish characters, all called Kelly and none related. Big Mouth Kelly had the contract for burying dead Chinese. Kelly the Rake was a professional gambler who dressed from head to foot in black, from his sombrero to his leather boots. Silent Kelly played solitaire all day, Molly Kelly ran a bawdy house, and Long Kelly worked for her.

I peered out into the darkness, but the Kellys were asleep, and had been so for some time.

And soon, so was I, as we fell through a land culled from the leafy meadows of an English shire, Dutch polders and subtropical rainforests, and were deposited in the city of Vancouver, just in time for breakfast.

Thirty-six

Vancouver, Saturday morning.

I am sitting by the window of a cafe in Gastown, nursing a mug of hot coffee and looking out at streets hissing with rain.

The way the rain opens plants, it seems to do with the past, bringing the sweet, sad smell of memory bursting into the damp air.

I am staying in a hotel down the street which has apparently been on its last legs since it opened almost a century ago. This morning the man came around spraying for cockroaches.

On top of the cistern in my room is a small clear plastic bag half filled with a white powder which I cannot identify.

I expect the drug squad to break down the door at any moment, demanding explanations which I do not have.

I finish my coffee and walk out into the hissing streets, leaving behind me a newspaper open at the casting ads placed by the city's film companies.

"Wanted: 55-65yrs Quebecois man, broken, agitated, charming and strange, to play Laporte in
Some Letters to a Young Poet," says the ad at the top.

The day passes on, and the sky clears. Now it is noon on Granville Island, where the beautiful people of Vancouver come down to the sea and play.

The rumour that they are rich is a downright lie. They are very rich.

In this little corner of God's green acre, even the Hell's Angels are freshly laundered as they spill onto Granville Island on a Saturday afternoon to wreak unlimited credit all around them.

Squeezing their gleaming Harley Davidsons into the space between the yachts and the convertibles, they stomp politely into The Pub to drink themselves sober on low-alcohol lager before heading back to the west of the city to park the bike back in the garage before it starts to rain.

On their way home, they will pass many small Chinese women driving German cars. These are the wives of the Hong Kong millionaires who are pouring into Vancouver before the handover in 1997, pushing average house prices past the £100,000 mark and forcing the beautiful people of Vancouver closer to the edge of the forests high on the mountains there, where the sun is already climbing to show that the day passes on.

Now it is three o'clock, in the 1,000 acres of Stanley Park, where the ordinary people of Vancouver come to play on a Saturday afternoon. In the zoo, the polar bear is asleep, the penguins amble back and forth like ancient butlers and a Japanese girl is playing a violin beneath a tree.

In 1942, the substantial Japanese population of British Columbia, many with Canadian citizenship and some of whom had fought for the Allies in World War One, was interned. Their possessions were sold to pay for the privilege, and in 1949 many of them were forced to emigrate to Japan.

But there is not even the ghost of a shadow of irony in her face, as she plays There's No Place Like Home. She looks up once, as a breeze from the ocean brings cherry blossoms fluttering down around her, but that is all.

On the grassy slopes below the zoo, two hundred people are watching Vancouver Rowing Club play Nanaimo in the finals of the British Columbia rugby championships.

On the balcony of the clubhouse, some of the wives have tired briefly of the game and have turned to watch a cricket match, munching silently on their hamburgers as they listen to the sweet click of willow on cork and watch the white figures run eagerly to and fro.

It is just like an English shire, except it isn't raining. They look anxiously at the sky, but the rain holds off, and the day passes on.

Now it is seven in the evening, and the steam clock in the centre of Gastown announces the hour with a gurgling eulogy into the humid night.

Down Water Street, two American tourists are buying a Coast Salish totem pole in Hill's Indian Crafts Shop for $7,500.

And around the corner, the bums are huddled in front of the TV at the Dugout Drop-In watching the hockey playoffs between the Montreal Canadians and the Hartford Whalers.

No drugs, No knives, No profanity, No sleeping, No fighting, No panhandling says the grimy notice above their heads.

Outside, two of the beautiful people are stopped briefly at traffic lights in their new yellow Mazda convertible. The hood is down, and the Rolling Stones are on the cassette player.

"You can't always get what you want, you get what you need," sings Mick Jagger, millionaire, to the beautiful people of Vancouver.

The lights change, and they drive away. The bums haven't raised their heads, and the rain comes at last, until you can hardly see them behind the steamy windows of the Dugout Drop-In.

The beautiful people stop down the street, put up their hood and drive home in their Japanese convertible, passing on their way a Chinese millionaire's wife driving a German car and a Canadian policeman riding an American motorcycle through the hissing streets of this little corner of God's green acre that is forever British.

Thirty-seven

I have tried to love Vancouver, and almost succeeded.

If cities were people, this one would be Oscar Wilde — self-consciously witty, hedonistic and
heading for a fall.

Witty because the call girls take Access, according to their ads in the newspapers.

Hedonistic because it's about the only place in the world where you can golf in the morning, sail in the afternoon and ski in the evening.

And heading for a fall because nowhere stays perfect for ever.

But this afternoon, as I walked through its wet, dappled streets and listened to Van Morrison's Brown Eyed Girl wafting out of dark cafes, and bought tiny, mysterious delicacies from Chinese bakeries, it was hard not to fall in love with Vancouver's indolent, satisfied soul.

Canadians already love it, of course. They emerge blinking from their endless, landlocked winters and come down to this Camelot by the waves to sniff the salt air and be astonished that flowers bloom in February.

And the rain! They love the glorious rain which washes down the dusty streets and drips from the trees which shelter every pavement.

Canadians don't have rain. In the prairies and the east, they seem to go straight from frostbite to sunstroke without the balmy, breezy days of spring. They even make a joke about it — that there are only two seasons in the country, winter and Labour Day.

But in British Columbia, they have so much rain that they export millions of gallons every year to
California.

And that still leaves plenty for the rest of Canada to come here, unfurl their umbrellas, and splash through the streets.

Or drive up to the mountains which rim the city, to see more water, in which salmon splash their way up through the rapids of Capilano Canyon to mate.

Or terrify themselves by walking across Capilano suspension bridge, a swaying curve of wood and rope hundreds of feet above the rushing river.

Or take the SkyRide cable car the 3,800ft to the top of Grouse Mountain, to stand in the clouds as they tear themselves to shreds on the rock and are reborn among the soft trees.

And then ride the Seabus across the harbour to Gastown for an aquatic encore, as the steam clock in Gastown sounds off the quarter hours with a misty chorus high into the damp air above the Gastown streets.

Time to sit and take a dry martini, it says, and look out at the bone-dry Canadians slowly blossoming as they walk to restaurants in the soft rain, and remember where they came from, where it rained all the time.

Time to think that maybe if I had $500,000 a year and an umbrella, I might love Vancouver after all.

But wait, I do have an umbrella!

Thirty-eight

What have King Edward VII, Richard Nixon, Shirley Temple, the King of Siam and I got in common?

They were all rich except for the last one.

And they all had afternoon tea at the Empress Hotel in Victoria, the capital of Vancouver Island which along with afternoon tea comes with other British institutions such as red double-decker buses, Marks (and Spencer), allotments, an opera house which actually makes money, and rain.

I arrived at the Empress to be greeted by Liba, the ferociously charming hostess. Turned out in several yards of Prince of Wales check, she stood guard at the entrance to the tea rooms beside a neatly folded pile of trousers and skirts for anyone foolish to turn up in jeans or shorts.

Czech she may be, but she guards the portals of her queendom against indiscretions of taste as zealously as any Devon dowager.

You get the feeling that if even Prince Philip wandered in wearing a God Save the Queen T-shirt and a pair of Levi's, Liba would politely zip him into a pair of the house grey flannels before letting him loose on Stan, one of the tea waiters, and five stone nothing of discreet Chinese efficiency.

"Ha! Eezstawbies," he announced, appearing at my side as I sat down with a pile of fresh strawberries and a silver bowl full of glutinous cream.

He set them down, but was back five seconds later with two large silver pots.

"Veyahspesh blen InyanChinese tea. Eezhowah," he said. I nodded sagely, and after he left peered in to find a very special blend of Indian and Chinese tea in one, and hot water in the other. Satisfied, I polished off my strawberries and cream in three glorious minutes.

No sooner had my empty fruit spoon tinkled to its final resting place than Stan pounced again. He was magnificent. He could hear a strawberry slide down a throat from 20 yards away and be there before it hit your stomach.

This time he bore one of those multi-layered cake stands that your rich auntie never left you when she died.

"Eezhoycrubb," he said, indicating with an elegant flourish two feathery slabs of crumpet soaked in the glistening eructations of a veritable squadron of bees.

"Eezmosa," he went on, his hand passing over a Swiss roll of smoked salmon nudging two peerless cucumber sandwiches.

Below these, on the bottom plate, rested an almost weightless scone the size of an elephant dropping, with ballast in the form of a pot of prime strawberry jam and a tub of clotted cream under which should have rested a slip of paper with the telephone number of the nearest cardiac unit.

On the very top plate, meanwhile, reclined a matching pair of pastries from which meandered the aromas of several English country gardens.

An hour later, a quite unremarkable sum of money changed hands, and I stepped weightily past a beaming Liba and an incomprehensible Stan to emerge replete onto the front lawn of the Empress.

Settling onto a wooden bench with a fine view of the bay, I watched the sun sink as my meal followed suit.

On the oak-clad hills behind me, the good citizens of Victoria drove their English cars home through residential areas where the average house price has nothing average about it.

On either side of the leafy avenues, manicured widows pottered about on their perfect lawns until they finally keeled over into the compost heap.

Far out in the glittering bay, a row of black spines unzipped the water, then fell again into the great deeps of the Pacific.

And so, with England behind me and whales in front, I sat there until the lights of Victoria flickered on, and the city announced that it was ready to receive visitors for the evening.

At last I retired to my room at the Ocean Pointe Resort, which boasted a magnificent spa whose vast range of treatments included one for firming up your bust. It's also open to women.

And the next day I went exploring an island which is about the same size as England, and is a combination of Devon, Bali and Paradise.

I could see why so many British naval officers retired here when they'd finished swabbing the decks, splicing the mainbrace or whatever it is they do in the Queen's Navy.

And why it had attracted thousands of Americans who realised that after they lived here for a few years they could claim Canadian citizenship, and with it free health care.

A few miles out of town is Fable Cottage, a fairy tale of a home built in the Fifties by local clothier Bernie Rogers and his wife Billie.

Sady, it was so unusual that people kept knocking at the door and asking for a look inside. The Rogers finally gave up and ran organised tours at weekends, hoping that interest would die down, but among the first to turn up for one were a writer and photographer for Beautiful British Columbia magazine, which ran a four-page picture special on the cottage.

Result – even more tourists, forcing the Rogers to move out of their dream home in 1972, and it's now open to the public, who wend their way down to it past mechanical gnomes cavorting in the gardens.

However, if it's gardens you're after, head to the other side of the island for 130 acres created by Jenny Butchart which would turn anyone's fingers green with envy.

Jenny was the wife of a cement tycoon, and although she knew nothing about gardening, when a friend presented her with some sweet peas and a rose in 1904 and she thought of turning a disused limestone quarry into a sunken garden.

Today, the sunken, Japanese, Italian and rose gardens have millions of amateurs drooling over the dahlias by day then gasping at the nightly firework display.

But by that stage I'd saved myself £180 by not buying one of the famous Cowichan sweaters (no, I'd never heard of them either) in the Native Heritage Centre and was on my way to the little town of Chemainus, which was just about to roll up the sidewalks in 1982 after its mill closed when local man Karl Schulz suggesting painting murals all over the place as a tourist attraction.

Artists from all over the world hauled out their paintbrushes when they heard of the project, and today Chemainus calls itself, with justifiable pride, The Little Town That Did. Heavens, even the mill has reopened.

Bernie and Billie Rogers would be glad to know that least some fairy stories have a happy ending.

Thirty-nine

It was the twilight time of day which the French describe with that wonderful word *crepuscule*, when the first gentle nudge of The Canadian freed us from the city.

I waited until the last twinkle of Vancouver had been swallowed by the dusk, then went to my room, broke the seal on a bottle of 12-year-old Canadian Club, and became more drunk than I care to remember. Just before I fell asleep, I wrote down a rhyming couplet which I thought at the time was wonderfully witty, but when I looked at it in the morning, all it said was:

"I've been up the Rockies, but I'd rather be at home in my sockies."

Gloomy with creative disappointment, I opened a new stick of deodorant which I'd bought in the Yukon. It was made in French-speaking Quebec, and was called English Leather, which gave me some hope for continuing Canadian unity.

A message on the label warned me that it was flammable until fully dry, so I switched on the little fan in the corner of the room and flapped my arms about for a minute. There's only one thing worse, after all, than your armpits bursting into flames, and that's when an Islamic fundamentalist jumps out and chops off your head as you're walking down the street minding your own business.

I went to the dining room and had steak and eggs for breakfast, which made me feel a lot better, and when I got back to the bedroom, the steward had changed the bed and the scenery.

The steward was wonderful. Earlier that morning, he'd knocked on my bedroom door and held up the Do Not Disturb sign.

"Did you hang this up?" he said politely.

"Well, yes."

"Oh."

He went away, looking puzzled.

After breakfast I went for a wander around The Canadian, which VIA Rail has spent a frightening amount of money restoring to the art deco elegance of its first appearance in 1955.

The outside is still the original shimmering snake of stainless steel, but the interior of the new Silver and Blue first-class section has been gutted and replaced with pastel shades, etched glass, pale leather and a series of murals by Canadian artists.

Sleeping accommodation is in a choice of suites, bedrooms, roomettes or bunks, and fine meals are served with a good wine list to the accompaniment of spotless linen and fresh flowers. That's what it says in the brochures, anyway, and it is, in fact, true.

Where most passengers spent the day, though, is at the back of the train, either in the mural lounge, the bullet lounge, or the observation dome watching Canada's restless landscape start to say something, then change its mind.

The second morning, the only occupants of the dome were Herb and Lou-Ann, a honeymoon couple from Louisiana who spent their days throwing bucketfuls of vowels over each other.

"Houane, Aey jes tol' am thayat wae jes lauv to cook in Looweeseeyana. Whaay, ma bes freyenshap eyas beyassed oan cookin', y'all know what Aey'm saeyin'?"said Lou-Ann.

In Looweeseeyana, it seemed, they had more hot spices in the food, more sun, more old-world charm, more down-home front porch friendship, more dogs called Old Blue and more festivals than anywhere else in the whole dang world.

"Whaay, we'all mus heyav teyan billion feyesteevals every mawnth eyan the summa," said Herb just before Lou-Ann confessed that they would have taken their honeymoon in Europe, except it would have meant all the hassle of getting passports.

Sick to the teeth of their naive, insular American boastfulness, I freed the killer fact which I keep ready to unleash on bores anywhere in North America — that in the UK most people get at least four weeks' holidays a year.

"Foowah?' wailed Lou-Ann, clutching Herb for support. But that was impossible. In Looweeseeyana, they only got two.

"I get five plus public holidays," I said, calmly twisting the fatal knife.

They marched off to their room shortly after, and I felt guilty for about half a second. But it was all right. After presumably singing a few verses of When the Saints Go Marching In, they emerged at five as sure as ever that Looweeseeyana was the center of the universe.

Five was the cocktail hour on The Canadian. The occupants of the lounges and the dome sipped their rye and soda or gin and tonic as the steward brought around hors d'oeuvres on a silver tray.

I sat in the mural lounge, sipping my Canadian Club and watching a video of Casablanca as the setting sun streamed in through the window blinds.

But I had missed the first 15 minutes, so at the end of the evening I was still the only person I know who has never seen the film. I'm saving it for something special, although I only have half a clue what.

As Ingrid flew off leaving Humphrey and me in tears, I rushed down to the dining car and was just in time for the last of the three servings of dinner, known on the train as the sunset, twilight and moonlight sittings.

I ordered the soup at 9.20, and it was 10.23 before it arrived.

Of course, the fact that we'd just crossed from Central Time to Eastern Time may have something to do with it. It could have been worse. If we'd been going the other way, I'd have paid for it before I'd eaten it.

Outside, in the moonlight, the land was waking and stretching after the long sleep of winter. On the lakes, the ice lay like patches of rippling silk the colour of gunmetal.

But Canada still had a few tricks to play. We had left Vancouver on a high summer day, and arrived in Jasper with the nip of spring still in the Rocky Mountain air.

Next morning, I pulled up my blind to reveal a winter wonderland of snow and silver birch in Northern Ontario.

I wouldn't have been surprised to arrive in Toronto to find the autumn leaves falling.

But that night, as I stepped onto the platform at Union Station, the moon was reflected in its mirrored skyscapers, uncertain and sad.

I felt the same way. I was sorry to say goodbye to my little room with its folding bed, its restless view rolling past my feet every morning and its little chrome switches for the lights and the five-bladed fan high in the corner.

I stood on the platform and listened to the distant trumpets of the city. There was no order in them, no welcome for someone who had grown to love the sleepy tickety-tack of paradise.

I shouldered my pack, and walked as slowly as I could into the real world.

Part Three

The East

Forty

It was just over a year since my journey to the west, and as the train hurtled from Toronto to Montreal, I held my breath for the moment when we all became French Canadian.

The moment when the atmosphere in the carriage suddenly became an ambience.

I looked out at golf courses carved out of the grassy wild, trying to spot the instant that the players started saying: "Merde!" instead of: "Heavens — missed again."

I studied back gardens, where men sat reading the Sunday papers by their swimming pools, trying to divine whether they were about to say: "Helen, throw me out a cold one there," or: "Helene, puis j'ai deux martinis sec, si'l vous plait?"

I even scanned the sky, waiting for it to darken from royal blue to French blue. But it was no use, especially when I was distracted by Bill.

He and his wife Hazel had been in France two years before, and accidentally got locked in a garden of one of the châteaux of the Loire one evening.

"I tell you, the only way out of that garden was over a 7ft wall with barbed wire on top. We got over OK, but I ripped my Tilley pants on the way down. Oh, those famous Tilleys," he said, chuckling to himself.

But somehow none of it rang true, and when Bill got off at Brockville, Hazel was nowhere to be seen.

Perhaps she was waiting in the car park, but it was very sad, the sight of him shuffling in his beige suit and training shoes past a man pushing a pram and a cloud of cigarette smoke before him down the platform past a cream and red sign saying: "Brockville: City of the 1000 Islands — Relocate to a Quality Community."

Its truth betrayed by its inhabitants, Brockville simmered in the sun as the train pulled out, the potential entrepreneurs in its first-class carriage mentally striking the town off the list of possible relocation sites for software plants and Cadillac franchises.

From the well-clipped greens outside town, Brockville's golfers watched the train go by with mournful eyes, as if they knew.

Above our heads, the sky darkened with rain, and soon we slid into Montreal.

I strapped accents to my vowels and went hunting for ambience in the drying streets.

Although most of the English-speaking minority who once owned 70 per cent of Canada's wealth left Montreal in 1976 after the election of the separatist Parti Québécois, signs and posters still hung everywhere in perfect Franglais — Grand Prix Nationale, Bar le Rendez-vous, Poulet Frit a la Kentucky — as if the city was being run by a crazed O-level French student.

Down in the old city by the harbour, painfully elegant people stalked the streets in search of the perfect bistro, couples sought each other in the shadows of horse-drawn caleches and moths tangoed to their deaths in the yellow light of ancient lamps.

Above them all, the new moon rose above the steel blue dome of the Bonsecours Market.

I went back to the hotel and spent five minutes in the bathroom, muttering into the mirror "Pas de bidet? Je suis désolé." (No bidet? I am desolate).

I tried sanity once, but it didn't agree with me.

Forty-one

Vancouver grew up to be a playboy, and Calgary became a cowboy.

Edmonton turned into an oilman, and Winnipeg a farmer. Toronto is a banker, and Ottawa is a politician.

But Montreal and Quebec, the twin godfathers of them all, still sit in the comfortable armchair of the east looking down on their errant offspring with a faint and weary sneer.

As well they might. When all the rest were forest, swamp and prairie, these two cities were already old.

Montreal was first settled in 1642 by Paul de Chomedey as a mission.

And even at the advanced ages of 325 and 334, the city was still fit and well enough to organise Expo 67 and the 1976 Olympics respectively.

Both left in their wake several pieces of architectural and financial flotsam which the city has had varying degrees of success in recycling.

Among the ones they don't like to talk about are the Olympic Stadium, originally called the Big O, then the Big Owe because it cost $700 million and wasn't finished until 11 years after the event, and now the Big Oh No because the roof is going to have to be replaced for another $50 million.

After an Olympics whose debts gave Quebec's provincial motto, Je me souviens — I will never forget — a new twist, Montreal, to its credit, learnt its lesson about using existing facilities for sporting events.

The Canadian Grand Prix track on Île Sainte-Hélène and Notre Dame Island, for example, is open to the public as a scenic drive all year, and in the week before the race is the site of the city's enthusiastic drivers queuing up for a slow motion preplay of the real thing.

And even sites like the futuristic Velodrome, built for the Olympic cycling events and rarely used since, have taken on a new life.

Or, in the Velodrome's case, a lot of new lives, of the assorted beasts which plunge, climb, swim, burrow and snooze in its four artificially created ecosystems — a tropical forest, Canadian woods, the St Lawrence underwater and the poles.

The Biodome, as it's called now, is all very impressive, and 1.25 million visitors have poured through its doors since it opened last June.

But I still suspect that places like this are just designer zoos.

Maybe it does give children a chance to see lynx and otters without getting eaten or holding their breath for 15 minutes.

But when you've stood six inches from an emperor penguin before you've even grown out of short trousers, what are you going to do for the rest of your life?

What's going to happen to your imagination? Or travel companies, for that matter?

I came out of the Biodome feeling a little like the catfish which was unaccountably swimming around in the piranha enclosure — full of admiration, but a little worried.

Perhaps it would have been better if they'd just left it as a velodrome, with a colony of breeding cyclists going round and round watched by groups of visiting penguins.

"Don't worry," one of the penguins would be saying to the other, "they were brought up in the Bronx, so this is like heaven for them."

Penguins like that would also appreciate another of Montreal's new attractions, the International Museum of Humour.

Sadly, when I went there I discovered that it was shut on Mondays — but then, it's rather appropriate that the sociable Montrealers don't feel like a laugh on Mondays.

115

Any good citizen will tell you that although those stuffy old Calvinist Anglos may have taken all the businesses to Toronto in 1976, when the separatist Parti Québécois came to power, they left the joie de vivre in Montreal.

"In Montreal we say TGIF — Thank God It's Friday — but in Toronto they say TGIM," a woman told me in a bar in the old part of the city down by the docks which, with its warehouse apartments, pavement cafés and trendy bistros, is where Montreal goes to play at the weekends when it's not sunbathing in the parklands and forests of Mont Royal above the city.

The old city is still where you'll find most tourists, too — wandering through the cobbled streets or peering up in admiration at the astonishing carved interior of Notre Dame Cathedral.

Just across the Place d'Armes is the almost as beautiful interior of the Bank of Montreal, although I'll have to take the locals' word for that, since I have an aversion to the inside of banks.

Just down the Rue Saint Jacques, once the rustling heart of Canadian finance, is the Molson Bank building, owned by the Scottish family who started the brewery in 1786.

Theoretically, owning a bank and a brewery seems like a perfect autonomous fiscal system, since your customers take their money out of one and put it in another.

Surprisingly, it didn't work, and the bank was taken over after the Second World War.

But then, Montreal has always had a rather strange relationship between commerce and spiritual matters like drink and religion.

In 1962, when it became apparent that Christchurch Anglican Cathedral was subsiding, a city developer jacked it up then decided to use the space he'd created underneath by building a shopping mall.

Today, that mall is part of a complex stretching for 18 miles, and Christchurch is possibly the richest church in the world, taking thousands of dollars in weekly rental from the shops below in a comfort able alliance between God and mammon.

Paul Chomedey, who founded Montreal to turn the minds of the Iroquois to God rather than fur trading profits, would not be pleased, but he would understand. After all, what can you expect from Anglicans?

Forty-two

For someone who had just come from well-scrubbed Toronto, Montreal Central Station crackled with the romance of dance hall tunes on an old radio.

It was the flickering lights, the names of the Grande Ligne trains.

And above all, the voice of the French Canadian announcer calling out the destinations like Saint -Hyacinthe in a voice so breathily seductive that you wanted to rush up to the control room and ask her to marry you and move there just so you could ask her to say "Saint-Hyacinthe" to you every night.

Sadly, while I was trying to work out whether this was entirely feasible or not, my train to New Brunswick was called and I was forced to contemplate the more mundane charms of my roomette.

Smaller than the bedroom I'd had on the journey west, this was a space 5ft by 4ft into which was miraculously fitted a folding bed, an armchair, an ingenious sink which emptied of water when you folded it away, a toilet, a drinking fountain, a luggage compartment, a toilet roll holder complete with soft toilet roll, a set of shelves, several coat hooks, two coat hangers, a pair of electrical sockets and a chrome fan.

There seemed to be only one problem. Since the room was only 5ft long, wouldn't the bed be the same?

But VIA Rail had already thought of that. When the bed folded down, the recess it came out of created an extra foot and a half.

It was astonishing. I was astonished. And what was even more astonishing was the landscape outside, all soggy woods and painfully green fields being devoured by arthritic cows.

It was just like home, except for the train, which was futuristic stainless steel outside and restored art deco inside.

It was like travelling through Monaghan in a spaceship designed by Charles Rennie Mackintosh, that well-known Scottish architect who also invented the waterproof indigestion tablet.

I folded myself into my folding bed, and didn't sleep at all, but somehow managed to wake refreshed.

I pulled up the blind and there was New Brunswick. It appeared to consist entirely of trees, although tragically there was no sign of Miss Nude New Brunswick from the lap dancing club in London, Ontario last year.

After some time a clearing came into view, filled almost entirely by a building called Holy Cross House.

Career opportunities in New Brunswick were, it seemed, somewhat limited.

You could either be a lap dancer, a lumberjack, or a nun with a temper.

Forty-three

I spit on your Taj Mahal, and mock your Great Pyramid of
Cheops. For I have seen the Famous Frog of Fredericton.

You have, naturally, already heard the story of Fredericton's
Famous Frog, but it bears repeating. One hippedy-hoppity morning
in the spring of 1880 something or other, Fredericton hotelier Fred
Coleman was fishing beside his home in Lake Killarney, New
Brunswick, when he caught a frog weighing 7lb 4oz.

When the freed frog showed no inclination to return to its
natural environs, Fred fed it some fresh bread and buttermilk he'd
brought with him for lunch.

The next thing he knew, the beast was turning up on his
front lawn almost daily looking for more. On that diet, he burgeoned
to a weight of 42lb and a height, including his back legs, of 5ft 4in.

Since steroid testing was not available in those less troubled
times, we shall never know whether the Fredericton Frog was the
Ben Johnson of its time. Indeed, it is only to be regretted that the
disgraced Canadian sprinter was not familiar with the benefits of a
bread and buttermilk diet.

We shall also never know what Mrs Coleman's reaction was
to her husband's increasing intimacy with a frog.

But we do know that before long the hopping hulk was
entertaining all and sundry by leaping over piles of orange crates and
bounding fecklessly after all the neighbourhood cats.

Within months he was a victim of his own fame, when
cabaret performances in cigar smoke-filled drawing rooms left him

with a ticklish respiratory condition. A frog in his throat, you might say, if you were that insensitive.

But before he could become the first ever specimen of Salientia, genus Anuran to perish from passive smoking, he was found floating belly-up in the lake where he had been discovered — the victim of fisherman who had dynamited the water.

The Famous Frog of Fredericton had croaked. He had hopped it to that great lily pad in the sky.

Frogless and inconsolable, Fred Coleman had his fat green friend stuffed, and stuffed he remains to this day, gazing out imperiously from a glass case in the York-Sunbury Museum in Fredericton.

Naturally, the frog is the highlight of a visit to Fredericton by anyone of culture, but there are, surprisingly, other things to see in the provincial capital of New Brunswick.

And a very pretty capital it is too, with a 208-year-old university, the Saint John River and lots of freshly painted wooden houses and public buildings in a sort of French revivalist neo-Gothic post-colonial style, if you catch my drift.

It was voted Canada's fittest city in 1983, and presumably because all the joggers picked up litter as they went along, the country's cleanest shortly after.

But the real reason the city looks so clean is that it was once the custom of the city's firemen, who were privatised and paid by the blaze, to burn down the buildings regularly, usually on a Friday night for drinking money.

However, since the fire brigade was taken over by the city council, that entrepreneurial spirit, and the Friday night fires, have died down.

Encouraged, the Frederictonians then started constructing more permanent buildings and changing the use of others.

The old opera house became the council chambers, which now stages monthly triviata instead of Traviata, under a selection of tapestries illustrating the history of the city.

These include Fredericton's version of the Mona Lisa — a horse whose eyes are said to follow you around the room — and a depiction of the ice man, who sold blocks of ice door to door in the summer. Few people realise that this custom is where the North American expression: "Have an ice day" comes from, probably because it's not.

If you like your art a little more expensive, however, you'll have to trot down the street to the Lord Beaverbrook Art Gallery.

Beaverbrook was brought up in nearby Newcastle, and this, the biggest art gallery on Canada's east coast, is only one of his gifts to the province.

Its centrepiece is Salvador Dali's Santiago El Grande, which had its bottom left hand corner whacked off when it was being shipped to the gallery.

The frantic Frederictonians wired Dali to come immediately and fix the damage, and a few weeks later a parcel arrived containing two tubes of paint, two brushes and the message: "Do it yourself. I'm busy."

Not that you'll hear that in the gallery, mind you. The best place to eavesdrop on yarns like that is five minutes' walk away in The Lunar Rogue.

The Rogue, twice voted one of the top 500 eating places in Canada, is named after Henry Moon, a local tailor who in the 1820s specialised in suits off the peg.

Someone else's peg, that is.

All you had to do was give Henry your measurements, then he'd follow someone home, break into their house and steal the suit.

All went well until a lawyer was admiring his favourite trousers at a dinner party when he realised he wasn't wearing them.

On Henry's way to jail in Kingston, he and the Fredericton constabulary were stopped by a fierce storm and struggled to a nearby inn, where Henry asked politely to use the outside toilet.

"I'm not going out in that," muttered the constable.

"Well, tie a rope around me and haul me back after five minutes," said Henry helpfully.

Showing a touching but on this occasion misplaced faith in human nature, the constable did as he was asked, and found when he tried to haul Henry in that the other end of the rope had somehow become attached to a barn door.

It's a shocking thing altogether, human nature, and in Fredericton the best way to get away from it is to hire a canoe for the afternoon to paddle across the Saint John and up the drowsy Nashwaak between maple bushes trailing in the still waters.

There, but for the watch on your wrist, you could be a voyageur three hundred years ago, your ears alert for the moccasin steps of Iroquois in the wood.

My fellow paddler for the afternoon was Kerry Smith, who had worked as a student minister in Newfoundland and Prince Edward Island and was now running Fredericton's Small Craft Aquatic Centre, where he kept talking about his staff, even though there seemed to be only one of them.

"So are you still going to be a minister?" I said.

"No. That's not part of the plan any more," he said, his eyes gazing wistfully into the secular middle distance.

Instead he was studying for a masters degree in psychology. Somewhere between the rocky shores of Newfoundland and the potato fields of Prince Edward, the rod of his belief had snapped, and now even his staff failed to comfort him.

His faith had gone the way of all things, frogs included.

Forty-four

New Brunswick must be the only place in the world where the natives happily admit that their biggest attraction is an enormous bore.

But then, tourism has always been a bit back to front in a province whose other charms include a magnetic hill near Moncton which cars apparently roll up, and waterfalls in Saint John which flow backwards.

The reason for the hill is an optical illusion caused by the surrounding land, although it does have its uses. The citizens of Moncton save so much petrol money rolling their cars up it that they can afford to go on three holidays a year.

The reason for the waterfalls is that huge tidal bore, when the famous tides of the Bay of Fundy come rushing in twice a day as if they'd just forgotten something important.

The bay is now almost compulsory on whistle-stop tours of the Maritime Provinces, and has led to the well-known expression: "If it's Fundy, it must be New Brunswick."

The tides shift 30 cubic miles of water every day, or as somebody with nothing better to do sat down and worked out once, the capacity of all the rivers in the world.

Or, to put it another way, the tide can rise higher than a four-storey house. So if you're ever building a house on the shore here, make sure it's at least five storeys.

Saint John itself, a former shipbuilding and fishing centre, is now more famous as the birthplace of actor Donald Sutherland, who presumably left because he couldn't stand the fog which it's also famous for.

According to Walter H Johnson Jr, an international travel expert quoted in Saint John's tourist literature: "Fog is an interesting difference in Saint John and can be a major attraction". Thank you Walter; and now, a little light music.

The city is more workmanlike than breathtaking, but it has a whiff of the exotic from its long association with the sea which is continued in the names on the stems of the big boats tied up in the harbour — Sea Guardian, Valletta, Ana Luisa, Rio de Janeiro, Renife, Panama — and is still worth spending a day in.

As you drive into town from the north, you'll pass the war veterans' hospital, which someone with poor geography and a worse sense of humour built opposite a graveyard.

Shortly afterwards, you'll come to the best place to see the city — the Carleton Martello tower, which was started in 1813 and finished in 1815 in readiness for the war against the United States.

Unfortunately, the war had finished in 1814, and the tower languished until the Second World War, when the Canadian government stuck a monstrously ugly lookout post on top. Still, at least this time they got it finished before the end of the war.

From the lookout post you can see Trinity Anglican Church, which has a fish on top of its 140ft steeple. The tides were unusually high that year.

You can see the Market Square, where on sunny days workers eat lunch on pavement cafés which come complete with witty waitresses — when you ask them for half a cup of coffee, they say: "Certainly sir — the bottom half?"

You can see Barbour's, which serves free dulse, that edible seaweed I'd previously thought only available in Northern Ireland, and recreates the inside of a general store from the last century.

And you can see Partridge Island, which opened as North America's main immigration and quarantine centre in 1785 and only closed in 1941, when it became a gunnery site.

Three million emigrants passed through here, 150,000 of them Irish and many of those fleeing the potato famine only to catch typhus fever on the ship and end their journey on a hillside grave with a fine view of the shores for which they hungered.

The descendants of the Irish emigrants who survived the ships and the island's 13 hospitals today make up two thirds of Saint John's population.

And the island itself, thanks to a 15-year battle by local man Harold Wright which has ruined his first marriage and his bank balance, is turning into an attraction which brings in thousands of visitors a year.

Harold and his volunteers have spent a decade uncovering the foundations of the island's 208-year history as immigration centre, lighthouse base and military complex, but with so little money and such an ardent desire to avoid Disneyfying it that they even refuse to cut the grass.

The result is wonderful, like a faded family scrapbook kept in an old ramshackle house.

People from Ireland come often to Saint John today to pay their $10, sail out in Harold's open boat, climb the grassy hill and stand at the door of the little museum with the bones of their ancestors beneath their feet.

And look down to the graveyards by the ocean, where a Mormon volunteer paints the white picket fence around the graves of Protestant and Catholic, Gentile and Jew alike.

Forty-five

Inspired by my successful hunt for the Famous Frog of Fredericton, I went in search of Painless Parker.

But since one should never rush into these things, first I was going to trek through the mighty forests of New Brunswick — and eat them.

Otherwise my chances of survival out there were not, it seemed, good.

Nancy Sears, the intrepid outdoorswoman who was to lead the way, had confided the night before that she had almost lost a travel writer in the dark last year and almost drowned another this year.

Why, only yesterday she'd been surprised by a black bear. Fortunately, the bear had been more surprised by her, and had run off in the other direction.

Even more fortunately, as we set off it began to rain, and all the bears with any sense were sitting in their caves watching old Yogi reruns on TV.

Relaxing slightly, I listened intently as Nancy explained to me the secrets of woodcraft.

"I go first," she said. "If I push a branch, I'll shout: 'Slapper'. If I see a hole, I'll shout: 'Sunker', and if I see an exposed root, 'I'll shout: 'Tripper'.

"What do I do if you see a bear?" I said, still unconvinced.

"Make sure you ran faster than me," she said generously, and off we set, slappering, sunkering and trippering our way through the mighty larders of New Brunswick.

It seems, you see, that you can eat just about everything in a forest except the trees and raw bears.

In the space of an hour, I'd tucked into purple and white violets, wood sorrel, beach peas and ostrich ferns.

Stuffed with undergrowth, as the rain poured down and the thunder rolled overhead, we plunged on past a waterfall and down a river.

It was like being 10 years old and playing Boy Scouts again. It was wonderful, apart from the fact that I'd come down with a bad case of woodsman's dyslexia, and was wandering around muttering: "Slipper, trapper, slonker, dumper."

All the same, I emerged from the mighty forests of New Brunswick feeling almost as rejuvenated as the party of six Jewish psychoanalysts Nancy took on the same trip a few months ago.

The highlight of the hike, they confessed to her afterwards, was being able to pee in the woods.

They were probably Freudians, I thought as we drove off and Nancy made the mistake of asking me what I wanted to do next.

"Take me to the house of Painless Parker," I said.

Edward Randolph Parker was possibly the most exciting dentist in the history of a profession whose members are not noted for their flamboyance.

A one-time carnival yanker of teeth, he built a chain of dental parlours across North America in the early years of this century, publicised by stunts like tightrope walkers between New York skyscrapers, marching bands and clowns.

Eventually growing tired of humans, he then established a reputation for pulling the malevolent molars of suffering lions and tigers, and on one occasion filled the tusk of a walrus with gold.

Unfortunately, his prolific public persona was not equalled in private, and he and his wife died childless, leaving their great white house on the hill to a servant girl called Ewing.

Today, Susan and Bobby Ewing live there, and five little Ewings run around the house between the legs of the grand piano, in front of a 15ft high chest with drawers filled with quill pens and inkwells, under oil paintings of sailing ships from St Martin's heyday, and past a huge trunk full of the half-models used to make those ships.

And sometimes, they go up to the top floor, where seven Parker daughters of the last century spurned needlepoint in favour of a rather more unusual hobby.

There, to this day, sit the dusty trophies of the skills of taxidermy: heron and owls, hawks and raccoons, their glassy eyes staring sightlessly out through the window to the woods where the black bears roam.

Forty-six

If God was a potato farmer, Prince Edward Island would be his home.

Some cynic once described the island as two beaches with a field of spuds in between, and like most cynics, they were wrong, for even the land here seems to have been brushed straight from paradise's palette.

Dirt roads the colour of wet rust, the trembling green of the fields, the bright wooden houses and white churches sleeping in laurel-dark woods, and the washed blue of the sky above all.

Even the grass seems freshly manicured, although if you ask an islander about it, you'll just get the answer that when they water the fields they put a little rum in so that the grass comes up half-cut.

Maybe what the cynic meant was that unlike the west of Canada, or much of the rest of the rugged east, the charms of this 140-mile long island off the New Brunswick coast don't walk up and smack you in the face.

You don't go: 'Wow!' in PEI, as you would in the Rockies. You go: 'Mmmmmm'; a feeling which the islanders bear out, for although they leave the island, they nearly always come back, giving the island the most stable population in the Maritimes.

It is, indeed, entirely appropriate that on the island which gave birth to one of fiction's most loved characters, that you should need a little of that which Anne of Green Gables valued above all else — scope for imagination.

The sort of imagination that, when the government was looking for ideas to get rid of the old Irving oil tanks at

Charlottetown, prompted one islander to write to the Guardian suggesting packing them with helium-filled ping pong balls and floating them somewhere else.

On the road from Charlottetown to West Point Lighthouse, for example, you will pass a simple white church with a sign outside saying Coleman Free Church of Scotland, but you won't find an interpretative centre explaining why it's there.

And in the Acadian Museum at Miscouche, you'll find one room spelling out how the original French colonists of the Maritimes were driven out by the British in the infamous deportation of 1758.

Three thousand Acadians were shipped back to France from PEI alone because they wanted to live in peace and refused to take an oath of allegiance to the crown. Seven hundred of them died when their prison ships sank in the English Channel, and many ended up in Louisiana, where their name eventually became Cajuns.

Not surprisingly, there are few smiling faces in the photographs of those who survived, either by returning to the island or by hiding in the woods. One Acadian family in New Brunswick who had saved the lives of their British neighbours by feeding them through a long hard winter were betrayed by the same family when spring came, for their land.

That is one room at the museum.

But there are two rooms where you have to bring your imagination: one room of artefacts in which stoves and brooms and tombstones are all piled in higgledy-piggledy, with no labels.

And one room in which there is a genealogy cabinet, with drawers holding 3,000 cards, each one bearing the name and sparse details about the Acadians of Prince Edward Island.

What scope there is in these little yellow, blue, green and orange cards, to imagine the life of Celestin Arsenault, to wonder what he hoped would become of his life as he grew up with his parents Joseph and Victoria, to wonder what he thought the first moment he laid eyes on Adoline Gauthier, who became his wife on February 12, 1866. Were there flowers of hope in his mind that day, and did they flourish or wither, in the rich red soil of his island home?

Bring your imagination, too, to the West Point Lighthouse, opened in 1875 and automated in 1963. Today Caroline Livingstone, the great grand-daughter of William 'Lighthouse Willie' MacDonald, runs the museum, restaurant and inn there, with nine bedrooms and not a right angle between them.

Bring your imagination for the memories of the days when rogues lured ships onto the rocks here using false lights, then murdered the survivors, whose bones farmers still turn up today with their ploughs.

Bring your imagination for the stories around the fire in the evenings of the ghostly burning schooner, which has been sighted off this shore many times over the last two hundred years. And the sea monster, 40ft long and looking like Nessie on holiday.

Both have been sighted as recently as last year by guests at the inn. There is no extra charge for seeing either.

You will need a little less imagination at Woodleigh, the home of Lt. Col. E. W. Johnston, a British Army officer who moved to the island in 1919 and proceeded to construct one-sixth scale replicas of famous British buildings.

Although the scale can be a little disconcerting, with 6ft high crows apparently bounding between St Paul's Cathedral and Ann Hathaway's cottage, Col Johnston's daughter Mary Elizabeth liked the chapel of St Peter-ad-Vincula in the Tower of London enough to get married there.

It was, I imagine, a small wedding.

You will need your imagination in the Eptek Sports Hall of Fame in Summerside, where you will find among the faded photos on the wall the story of local baseball, ice hockey, golf and rugby star Paul Jay, who according to the newspaper clippings beside his lean face, was only sent off once, for "acting like a Protestant".

There's only one more stop for your imagination, in Belfast, which was the site of the 1847 riots over changes in the voting system.

Today it is the grassy scene of a few white houses and St John's Presbyterian Church (minister Rev Roger MacPhee, organist Mrs Frances McBurnie, Clerk of Session Sinclair MacTavish).

It was a Sunday morning, and Rev MacPhee, a dapper man in a matching black suit and moustache, was inside getting things ready for the Lord.

Outside, his Ford truck was sitting in the car park with the keys in the ignition, as obvious an indication as can be that he has never visited the scene of the other Belfast riots.

Or, in the spirit of Anne of Green Gables, that he uses his imagination for more positive things.

I had only read the book the day before, on the bus from New Brunswick, sitting behind a driver wearing a shoulder patch proclaiming 14 years' safe driving, which meant that the odds were stacking up against him mightily and we would be lucky to reach Charlottetown alive. I'd have been much happier if the patch had declared: "Wrote the bus off yesterday. Three injured."

I cried when I read the book, and quite right too. If men cried more often, women wouldn't need to cry so much.

On the island itself, you won't meet anyone who would like to string Anne Shirley up by her red
pigtails, but quite a few who'd like to break a slate over the head of whoever dreamed up Anne's Diner , Anne car number plates, the Anne Shirley Motel, Matthew's Market and Marilla's Pizza.

There was even Anne's Riverboat, a cafe in the shape of a Mississippi steamer, a leap of genres which either requires a great deal of imagination or a course of hallucinogenic drugs from Anne's Pharmacy.

At the house which Lucy Maud Montgomery used as the model for Green Gables, there is, of course, a gift shop where you can buy Anne hats, mugs, plates, teddy bears, dolls, paintings and sweatshirts.

Still, we should be grateful for small mercies. It could have been called Ye Olde Greene Gables Gift Shoppe.

Outside the house itself stood several young Japanese women, their faces wide with joy as they looked up at the door into their childhood dreams, hardly daring to step inside.

The book is a compulsory text for Japanese 13 and 14-year-olds, and they have grown so infatuated with Anne that they come here in their thousands every summer; to faint or burst into tears, to gaze at the bed upon which Anne flung herself in despair when she was told she couldn't go to the picnic, to peer into the oven from which Anne proudly drew her layer cake accidentally flavoured with liniment oil instead of vanilla.

And they arrive at the house where Lucy Maud Montgomery grew up, to be married in the room where she was married in 1911, in front of the same fireplace and to the same old Presbyterian hymn, The Voice That Breathed O'er Eden, on the same organ.

On their right, through the window, they can see the Lake of Shining Waters, and on their left, if they turn slightly, they can see themselves in the glass front of the enchanted bookcase, entering with their new husband the world of flowers and sunshine and fairies that Anne imagined behind that glass.

Margaret Attwood, the Canadian writer, has suggested several theories why the Japanese love
Anne so much — her exotic red hair, her refusal to lose her identity, her breaking of taboos, her dedication to study and love of nature.

But Anne would probably say that maybe it's because she helped give them the imagination which makes them turn up at Green Gables and ask to see her grave.

And Anne would probably be disappointed at what has become of Green Gables, which seems to change everything that you imagined.

Perhaps you dreamed that the house would be in a hollow, and it is upon a hill.

You imagined that Anne's bed was on the left of her room, but it is on the right. You imagined walls and bare floors, and find floral wallpaper and designer sisal matting.

You imagined that the kitchen will be sparse, and find 12 matching beer glasses.

You imagined that you will see the haunted wood from the front door, and you see the ninth hole of the Green Gables golf course.

If you walk to the edge of the lawn, though, you will see the wood, where "Anne, on her way to the Orchard Slope, met Diana, bound for Green Gables, just where the mossy old log bridge spanned the brook...where tiny ferns were unrolling like curly-headed green pixie folk wakening up from a nap."

"It's...It's kinda neat, isn't it," said the brain-dead American woman behind me to her husband.

But then, when I went alone in the wood, a spruce branch creaked in the breeze, and even on a bright summer afternoon, my heart leapt.

Anne is alive, in the imagination, where she always wanted to be, and where she belongs.

Forty-seven

Urban Carmichael is a cultural development officer with the Prince Edward Island government by day, and a combination of Ayrton Senna and Daniel O'Donnell by night.

It was a Saturday evening, and Urban was driving me to Rainbow Valley, a country amusement park, where he was to sing.

Elsewhere on the island, each of his nine brothers and sisters was also performing that night.

It was his fourth engagement of the day, and after it he would drive back to Charlottetown for another one. The next morning he was taking the boat to Halifax for a similar day, then coming back to start work on Monday morning.

It was a sunny evening as we drove to Rainbow Valley, with Urban talking at the speed of a man who didn't have long to live.

That was probably because his dodgy Audi was in the middle of the road most of the time, with the brake light permanently on, the speedometer thankfully broken and Stompin' Tom Connor on the stereo.

"Do you know Hal Roach? Do you like Garth Brooks? Have you heard of Angèle Arsenault?" he shouted over the roar of the wind through the sunroof as a woman in a station wagon pulled out in front of us without looking.

"Beautiful countryside around here," he continued for no apparent reason as he swerved around her without reducing speed. "Wouldn't want to move out to the prairies. Takes your dog four days to get lost out there. What do you think of Rita MacNeil?"

I was terrified, not so much by the prospect of death, but by the thought of what he'd do to me if he found out that I listened to classical music.

My body would be washed up on the southern shores of the island in a couple of months, weighed down with Dolly Parton tapes.

My luggage would be shipped home slowly. On my laptop computer, the little battery warning light would blink on somewhere in the middle of the Atlantic, and slowly, in the darkness of a ship's hold, the memory would fade and die, taking with it the written but unsent tales of the Famous Frog of Fredericton, Painless Parker of St Martin's and how to eat the mighty untamed forests of New Brunswick.

But all was well. We got to Rainbow Valley without me having to convince Urban that Grieg, Sibelius and Tchaikovsky were a trio of itinerant Galway fiddlers, to find a red London bus with Heathway & Wood Lane via Tottenham on the front disgorging a party of speed skaters' parents from all over Canada into a huge barn.

Urban established himself on the stage at one end, directly opposite his rival for the attention of the speed skater's parents – a pile of boiled lobsters.

It was like the end of High Noon, with Urban as Gary Cooper and dead crustaceans lurking behind the saloon windows, their feelers edging back the curtains and their tiny black eyes peering down the dusty street for a bead on The Coop.

Urban settled onto his seat, squinted at the lobsters and began. His speciality was asking people where they were from, then making up a song about it.

"Winnipeg? I thought Winnipeg was a game show for pirates," he would say, before launching into "Winnipeg, it's a great old town, They never turn the maple leaf upside down."

That sort of thing, and they loved it. But then, the lobster wasn't ready yet.

Unable to stand the tension as the showdown neared, I wandered outside and found myself looking across the lake at another of Rainbow Valley's attractions, the Ripley's Believe It or

Not! Museum, and walked across to take a look. It was shut, Believe It or Not!

From the other side of the window, a photograph of a grinning African man looked back at me, three tennis balls in his mouth.

Behind me, a fat moon rested on the top of the No 175 bus to Tottenham, and the sound of Urban singing: "I'm a three-legged man, with a two-legged woman, being chased by a one-legged fool" rose into the still, cold night.

But it's not easy applauding with a lobster claw in each hand, and Urban was subdued as we drove home later.

I could tell by the way he stopped for red lights.

Forty-eight

Prince Edward was a pleasant sort of chap — self-centred, spendthrift and much given to flogging and hanging his soldiers.

However, he did have one saving grace — he fell in love.

The son of George III had met Alphonsine-Thérèse-Bernardine-Julie de Montgenêt de Saint-Laurent while he was commanding the garrison in Quebec.

Realising that declaring any affections he might have for her would take all night, he called her simply Julie, and promptly fell in love. She did as well, which is always helpful.

Since he was a Protestant prince and she was a Catholic commoner, marriage would have been about as likely as the Pope knocking on the door of the Paisley residence one dark and stormy night to enquire about the chances of applying successfully for the hand of Rhonda.

But love is love, and when Eddie was sent to Halifax, the capital city of Nova Scotia, in 1794, Julie came too.

After finishing his day job of building a star-shaped citadel against possible French invasion, Edward would round up all the troops he hadn't flogged and hanged, and set them to work landscaping the grounds of the royal love nest to the north of the city, cutting paths out to form the letters of Julie's name and digging a pond in the shape of her heart.

If you look at the rather attenuated shape of the pond today, you will notice that anatomy, either romantic or practical, was not Edward's forte.

And neither, sadly, was fidelity in the face of the enemy.

He was ordered home in 1800, and Julie ended her days in a Belgian convent, probably praising the strength of the beer and cursing the weakness of men.

Edward married the Prussian princess Mary Louise of Saxe-Coburg, and in 1819 they had a child which they called Victoria.

It is, at least, appropriate that when their little girl grew up to be Queen she gave her name to an era in which duty came before passion.

Julie wasn't the only well-known victim of love's labour's lost in Halifax.

In August 1863, a woman calling herself Miss Lewley arrived in the city searching for a man she said was her cousin, Lieutenant Albert Pinson, who was stationed in the citadel.

In fact, she was Adele Hugo, the daughter of Victor, and Lt Pinson wasn't her cousin, but the object of an obsession which drove her to follow him to social events and plague him for the next three years, carrying with her an opened black silk umbrella, rain or shine.

In a stream of letters to her mother, she said that she had married Pinson, but a series of petty squabbles was forcing them to separate.

In 1866, Pinson's regiment was posted to Barbados, and Adele followed him there, but was forced to return to Paris in 1872, where she died in 1915, still insisting that she was Mrs Pinson.

Halifax, for some reason, seems to attract misplaced love affairs.

Three years ago, a young Japanese woman who had got on the wrong plane landed at the city's airport and wandered around muttering the only English words she knew: "Anne of Green Gables" to everyone she met, under the mistaken impression that she was on Prince Edward Island, where Lucy Maud Montgomery wrote that most famous of children's books.

A burly taxi driver finally took pity on her and got her packed off on a plane to PEI.

Today, few people remember the tale of either Adele Hugo or the young Japanese woman in Halifax, but the sad, sweet tokens of Edward and Julie's lost love are still to be seen — the pond, the foundations of the home at Hemlock Ravine which they named Friar

Laurence's Cell after Romeo and Juliet, or the beautiful clock tower whose workings he later bequeathed to the city.

And in the citadel which he was sent there to build, there hangs today a portrait of him.

I looked at it for a long time trying to work out who he reminded me of, with his balding head, his amiable but slightly hyperthyroid gaze and his well-padded jowls.

And then it finally came to me. The Famous Frog of Fredericton, of course.

Poor old Edward. The only prince in history to be kissed by a beautiful woman and end up looking like a frog.

Forty-nine

Otis looked like WC Fields, and regarded facts as a starting rather than a finishing point.

As well he might. When I'm 76, I probably won't know a fact if it walks up and hits me on the nose.

Otis, a retired Canadian Army lieutenant and flat roof inspector, was to be my guide for a tour around historic Halifax.

And within minutes it became clear that the facts were not going to get in the way of either a good story, or Halifax's place in the great scheme of things.

"Over there is Point Pleasant Park, the only park in North America within city limits," said Otis with an insouciant wave as we drove past several acres of dappled glades.

"What about Stanley Park in Vancouver?" I said.

"It's a beautiful park," said Otis, cleverly sidestepping the question.

"But surely it's inside the city limits."

''It's... just on the outskirts," said Otis, looking so crestfallen that I decided to keep my mouth shut as he pointed out King's College as the oldest university in Canada, founded in 1789.

Hold on, Otis, didn't the universities of New Brunswick in Fredericton and Georgia in the USA both claim to have been established in 1785?

Who cared? Otis wasn't the only one to suffer from flexibility of history- earlier in the day I'd seen a book proudly claiming Halifax as the birthplace of actor Donald Sutherland, an honour claimed with equal pride by Saint John in New Brunswick.

Only God and Donald's mother knew the truth, but it was becoming obvious that the tour with Otis was going to be an adventure up the river of the past, with truth lurking back there somewhere in the trees, dangerous and intangible.

"Bet you didn't know that the swans in the public park over there were donated by KLM," said Otis.

I certainly didn't, and I had no particular reason to doubt it. I asked him if they flew to Amsterdam twice a day, and got half a smile for my efforts.

"And up here is the famous clock tower which Prince Edward bequeathed to the city. Until it was cleaned last year it hadn't stopped since 1799," said Otis, gaily ignoring the fact that Edward had only sent the working parts over in 1803, as a token to the city where he had spent several wonderful years with his mistress, Julie Saint-Laurent, before being forced to go home and father Queen Victoria.

"I believe Prince Edward came here from Barbados," announced Otis.

It was, actually, Quebec, but the day was becoming far more interesting than if Otis had been right all the time. It was turning into a battle of wits, in which each fact he handed me was held up to the light and inspected for signs of truth before being either tossed aside or written down.

"We're just coming up to the Citadel," said Otis as we drove up to the star-shaped and virtually impenetrable fortress built between 1828 and 1856 because of the threat of a French attack which never came.

"This is the most visited historic attraction in Canada, and those are students dressed in the uniform of the 48th Highlanders," Otis declared, getting out of the car and lighting a Du Maurier.

"Second most visited historic attraction after Green Gables House, 78th Highlanders," I wrote in my notebook as we embarked on a fascinating but depressingly factual 50-minute audio-visual history of the city.

The Citadel has been painstakingly restored by Parks Canada, whose muted beige and dun uniforms are presumably designed to blend into the landscape.

This can be very disconcerting, like when you're walking past a grassy verge and it suddenly leaps up and starts talking to you.

"Say, you're a big guy. You must be seven feet three," said Otis as I walked along checking clumps of grass for life.

"Actually, I'm six seven, Otis," I said, sure that I would end up seven feet three, no matter what I said.

As we left, the students of the 78th were preparing to fire the noon gun, traditionally used by ships' captains in the harbour to synchronise their chronometers. As Otis pointed out in a disappointing lapse into truth, it is the second largest natural harbour in the world after Sydney.

At one time the gun was once also fired at 9.30pm, to remind soldiers that they had half an hour before curfew.

Since many of them were directly below the Citadel in the red-light area around Brunswick Street, happily infecting themselves with what the armed forces coyly refer to as "self-inflicted injuries", they didn't have far to run home.

Halifax, which still employs 10,000 people at its navy base, was a city built on war, and one which never seems to know what to do with itself robbed of the glamour of a uniform and the dark romance of distant guns.

But the Citadel was never attacked, and Halifax's function in the First World War was repairing ships and waving goodbye to soldiers as they set off for the Western Front.

Until a cold, clear morning in 1917, when the city's role as an abandoned war bride finally came to an abrupt and shocking end.

On December 6, the Imo freighter — built in Belfast and formerly the Runic cargo liner of the White Star Line — collided with the French cargo ship Mont-Blanc, which was carrying 35 tons of benzol, 300 rounds of ammunition, 10 tons of gun cotton, 2,300 tons of acid and 400,000lb of TNT.

The subsequent explosion laid waste to a third of Halifax, killed more than 2,000 people and injured 9,000. The shock wave was felt 270 miles away. It was the biggest man-made explosion before the nuclear age.

Two hundred of the victims, who had gathered in a common on the other side of the Citadel for safety, froze to death that night as the worst blizzard for years hit the city.

The explosion is the subject of a moving exhibition at the Maritime Museum of the Atlantic, where you will also find artefacts from the Titanic, including the ship's original distress signal and photographs of the dead being brought aboard the Halifax cable ship Mackay-Bennett. The second- and third-class bodies had a tag strung onto their big toes, but the first-class corpses were embalmed and placed in coffins.

Quite right, too. No point in paying all that money for a first-class ticket if you can't get embalmed.

"This here's supposed to be the captain's deckchair," said Otis, who had been strangely quiet for several minutes.

To the north of the city, in Fairview Cemetery, you will find the graves of over 150 of the Titanic's victims.

The headstones are simple granite slabs bearing the names of those who lie beneath and the same, cold date repeated time after time — April 15, 1912.

Some, like those of the crew who stayed at their posts, are embellished with heroic verses: "Everett Edward Elliott, Aged 24. Each man stood at his post, While all the weaker ones went by, And showed once more to all the world, How Englishmen should die."

But the most poignant ones of all are the graves of victims like Alma Paulson, who was 29 when she died with her four children, aged between eight and two. Her surname was actually Pålsson, but it hardly matters.

Her husband Nils had emigrated from Sweden to Chicago in 1910 to work as a trolley car operator and save enough money for third class tickets for Alma and their four children, eight-year-old Torburg, Paul, six, Stina, four, and Gosta, two. All were lost.

Or the others simply dedicated: "To the memory of an unknown child". What lost futures there are, in those words.

After all the death associated with Halifax, it's usually wise to end any tour of the city with a visit to Province House, the seat of provincial government and a barrel of laughs.

Here hang the portraits of men like Joseph Howe, the editor of the Nova Scotian, who was tried for libel in 1835 for accusing the government of corruption and stealing public money.

Unimpressed with his lawyers, Howe studied law for three weeks and defended himself successfully in a six-hour speech which established the principle of the freedom of the press.

Province House was also the home of a series of magnificently carved plaster falcons above each door.

Until 1839, when Sir Laurence O'Connor Doyle arrived.

Sir Laurence, an Irishman and fervent anti-American, became convinced that the falcons were bald eagles, and lashed out at 11 of them with his cane, leaving Province House with Canada's finest collection of headless falcons — a fact which even Otis would not dispute.

Otis had spent the tour of Province House hovering in the background, having handed me over to Kathryn Roddis, who had a disturbing belief in accuracy for one so young.

But the ghost of Otis' ancestors haunted the building. On one wall, portraits of King George I and Queen Caroline hung side by side.

The paintings arrived in the 1840s labelled George II and his wife Caroline, and it was not until 1964 that a sharp-eyed librarian spotted that the one on the left was actually George I, Caroline's father-in-law.

It was no wonder that Otis looked happy as we drove back to the hotel.

"You still drive on the right at home, eh?" he said.

"No, the left, Otis," I said.

"Oh? It's been changed since I served there in the war, then."

"No, it was always on the left."

"Are you sure?"

I said goodbye to Otis, then ran into him half an hour later in a nearby pub.

He sat down, lit a Du Maurier and started to tell me about all the things he'd forgotten earlier. Facts whizzed past my ears and flew through the open window.

Outside in the street, untethered by corroboration, they were slowly blown north by a fresh sea breeze.

After lunch, Otis shook my hand and got up to leave.

"Afternoon," he said.

I checked my watch as he walked away, just to make sure it was.

Fifty

Like most Dutch people, Andre and Reni were nine feet tall and looked like they'd just been sandblasted clean.

I'd met them the night before in Halifax, Nova Scotia, at a ceilidh in the Hilton.

Now, there may be those of you who subscribe to Sir Seamus Newton's Fourth Law of Motion, that it is physically impossible for a ceilidh and a Hilton to occupy the same space.

But Andre and Reni were enjoying it. When I met them, they were dressed from head to foot in matching Caballero T-shirts, jackets, trousers and shoes.

At first I thought this was because they were labouring under the delusion that this was fashionable, but it turned out to be because they had won a prize in a Dutch TV show and were sponsored by Caballero.

Their reward was to travel around the world in 30 days looking for buried treasure. The four other winners were simultaneously dancing, sporting, sleeping and volcano-hunting their various ways around the planet. The winner would get a trophy and about £4,000.

Andre and Reni were 22 days through their trip, and had already been to Mauritius, Reunion and the Seychelles, and were now on their way to Oak Island off the south coast of Nova Scotia, allegedly the site where Captain Kidd buried his treasure in a deep cave.

Three boys had almost discovered it in 1795, but disturbed the booby-trapped platform that it was sitting on, sending it plummeting a further 230ft and leaving it underwater.

A syndicate of Canadian and US businessmen have since lowered a TV camera into the pit, where they claim to have seen the treasure chests and a severed human hand, but they're still scratching their heads about how to drain the cave to get it out.

As for me, I was driving west in the fog on my way along the coast from Halifax, a city I had left in the grip of terminal firstitis.

This is a common ailment among Americans, who with none of the larger banknotes of history in their possession, scrabble in their pockets for the small change.

Now it has struck Canadians too. The day before, I had been variously informed that Halifax was the home of Canada's first English-speaking settlement, Protestant church, newspaper, telegraph system by flag, Sunday school for blacks, decorated Christmas tree, visit of Charles Dickens and wife, North American church built in one day by 2,000 people and ice hockey and basketball games.

I'd even caught it myself, wandering around telling complete strangers that the News Letter, the paper I worked for, was the oldest English language newspaper in the world.

Why, that morning I'd leapt out of bed after realising that it was the first time I'd ever slept in Halifax, and rushed into the corridor to see if someone had erected a plaque pointing this out to passing chambermaids.

But no. It was a disappointed man who drove west towards Peggy's Cove, past abandoned snowmobiles on front lawns. With the sorrowful eyes of their damp round headlights, they looked uncommonly like the portrait I had seen the day before of Prince Edward, who in his turn had looked uncommonly like the Famous Frog of Fredericton.

Frogs and fogs. Was there no end to it all, I thought grimly as I arrived at Peggy's Cove, which has probably swallowed up more Ektachrome than anywhere else in Nova Scotia.

This archetypal Maritimes fishing village has a population of 60, most of them seagulls.

It has a little dock with real fishermen and a little souvenir shop with artificial souvenirs. Including plastic frogs, naturally: squeaky ones, for $3.99.

"Fishing boat's in," said the manageress to the girl behind the cash till as I was inspecting the frogs to see if they resembled Prince Edward as well.

"I've seen fish before," said the girl glumly, flicking over page 37 of Seventeen magazine to find that Craig was taking Gabby to the prom even though he'd promised Anna, the brute.

Peggy's Cove is lovely, but it would be more lovely if nobody knew about it for a while. The tourist board should put up signs saying: "On no account go to Peggy's Cove; it's too dull for words."

Then everyone would turn up and declare: "But heavens, it's gorgeous!"   ·

As indeed is all the Lighthouse Route past Mahone Bay, with its trinity of church spires marking the border between the dark forest and the glittering sea.

There was a little Titanic museum here, but it has now gone the same way as the ship.

As did the Bluenose, the legendary schooner built in 1921 in Lunenburg which won every race in sight, but ended her days in ignominy when her owners failed to raise the money to preserve her.

Her masts hacked off and an engine installed, she broke up and sank after hitting a coral reef off the Haitian coast in 1946. A replica, the Bluenose II, now hauls tourists on daytrips out of Halifax.

Lunenburg today is a beautiful town of carpenter gothic and widows walks, where you can still find the yard which built the Bluenose and visit a comprehensive and interesting fishing museum.

There, you can look at photographs of whales being hunted, and wonder what exactly the expression "Having a whale of a time" is supposed to mean.

Not to mention wondering why the museum has put up signs saying Watch Your Head on all the stairs.

How can you watch your head when your eyes are in it?

It was a problem which occupied me all afternoon, as I paddled around the islands off the coast in a bright yellow kayak, feeling like the merman who grew a banana for a tail.

There can't be a better way to see these islands than from three feet up, sniffing the air and listening to the sounds of the water and the woods.

And then driving home as the sun boils the rain off the roads and the glassy inlets, so that you feel as if you've left the earth and are moving through the clouds where no frogs live.

Fifty-one

On the way north from Lunenburg, I passed from time to time white wooden fire stations in the forest, with the red engines sitting out the front looking as if they'd come straight from the toyshop.

And the first pawn shop I'd seen in Canada, a nation not noted for its poverty.

It was mostly filled with junk, but under the glass counter was a beautiful Victorian amber and silver necklace.

"Only 90 bucks," said the owner, a man who looked as if he was just trying out optimism for size. "Nobody's coming back for that one."

But I didn't believe him. After Otis in Halifax, I didn't believe anyone any more.

The necklace could have been an heirloom which the father of a poor family had pawned last week so he could give his wife her first romantic night out for 40 years, and I could just imagine the conversation when he returned to the shop to reclaim it.

"You sold it! But you promised, you... Emily will never forgive me. Her grandmother's necklace!"

I left it there, since I've enough problems without Emily's broken marriage on my hands, and continued north, along roads once travelled by Joseph Howe, the patrician editor of the Nova Scotian and later governor of the province.

Howe, who tramped around much of Nova Scotia from 1828 to 1830 trying in vain to collect money from the papers debtors, wrote about his travails in the book Western and Eastern Rambles.

The roads were so bad then that one farmer who had driven from Windsor to Liverpool to sell cheese sold his cart and rode back a different way because he couldn't face the journey home.

The inns weren't much better. Captain William Moorsom, a contemporary of Howe's, reported that one boarding house was "a shabby one-storey cottage with broken windowpanes, the innkeeper an unshaven and sinister looking backwoodsman, the main dish broiled salt mackerel and potatoes, and the bed chamber a draught-swept cell with a filthy truck-bed."

Then, inns were classified according to whether they served white sugar, brown sugar or black molasses.

Even a man of Howe's foresight would have had difficulty taking in the scene today as I finished off my waffles with home-made blueberry sauce and freshly ground coffee, then jumped into the rental car, set the cruise control and air conditioning, and vanished into the morning at 62.5mph and 17.5C respectively.

Until I hit the roadworks, with a man at either end holding up those swivelling Slow and Stop signs, which always worry me immensely.

What would happen if both men were psychopaths who painted Go Faster! on their signs then held them up at the same time?

Disaster, that's what.

It was a miracle that I got to Middleton alive and saw the signs for Route One to Wolfville — what a wonderful sound that had to it. You could make a country and western song out of it, if you were that way inclined.

My woman's gone and left me and my horse is dead
My mom's become a hippy and my dad's turned Red
But deep inside my cowboy heart, I cain't help feel a thrill
Cos' the past and I will always part,
Down that good ole road to Wolfville

Chorus: Route One to Wolfville, Route One to Wolfville
I'm on that good ole road again
Down Route One to Wolfville.

Mmm. It needed some work, especially since I kept singing the first verse to the tune of Help me Rhonda.

Middleton and Wolfville are on the Evangeline Trail, named after the heroine of Longfellow's epic poem.

It also has a number of other diversions, like Howard Dill.

Howard, four times the world pumpkin growing champion, answered the door in his socks when I knocked.

A spare, mild man with pale blue eyes and a tanned face, he had been sitting in the kitchen of his home in Windsor totting up the weekly accounts in an old ledger book, surrounded by sleeping kittens and trophies from the World Pumpkin Confederation for his 800lb monsters.

From the wooden table in this kitchen he runs a business exporting giant pumpkin seeds to dozens of countries.

He's sold over seven million seeds to the Japanese, which probably explained why I'd seen so many of them on Prince Edward Island. No room at home, with all those pumpkins.

His secret, he said, was good seeds, soil and sunshine, and the reason he did it was to make people happy.

"There's something about a pumpkin that makes folks smile, and the bigger the pumpkin the bigger the smile," he said as a white kitten lying on the accounts book woke up, opened one blue and one green eye, and dozed off again.

"Any chance of seeing a pumpkin?" I said.

"Sure. Just hang around till August, when they grow," said Howard helpfully.

Half an hour down the road from Howard's pumpkin patch is Uniacke House, named after Richard John Uniacke.

Richard, the disinherited son of Protestant landed gentry in Cork, emigrated in 1774 and married Martha Delesdernier, the 12-year-old daughter of his Nova Scotian employer. Martha eventually bore 12 children and, hardly surprisingly, died when she was 40.

In 1776, Uniacke was arrested for alleged American sympathies. As he was being brought to Halifax, he saw and noted the piece of land which caught his eye.

The charges against him were dropped, and within five years he was Solicitor General for Nova Scotia.

In 1815 he built an eight-bedroom mansion on the 100-acre site he had spotted on his ignominious way south, and today it is open to the public, with its original furnishings.

But until Route One to Wolfville is renamed the Dill or the Uniacke trail, most people will still drive it to Grand-Pré, the source of Longfellow's poem about the British expulsion of over 10,000 French Acadians from Nova Scotia in 1755.

The tragic heroine of the poem, Evangeline Bellefontaine, is about to wed Gabriel Lajeunesse when the British announce the deportation order.

Put aboard transportation ships for Louisiana with only what they can carry, they become separated.

For many years Evangeline searches for her lover, until she finally admits defeat and joins the Sisters of Mercy in Quebec. Nursing wounded French soldiers after the city has been besieged by the British, she suddenly recognises a dying soldier as her Gabriel.

The shock causes her death, and when Gabriel dies, the two lovers are laid to rest, together in death as they could not be in life.

At Grand-Pré, a church was built in 1922 on the site of the church of Saint-Charles-des-Mines, where the British announced the deportation order then burnt the church and the Acadians' homes to prevent them returning.

Inside, the story of the forced exodus is told in paintings by Claude Picard, and outside is Philippe
Hebert's famous sculpture of Evangeline.

The right side of her face is that of a young, innocent woman, but as you walk around it is supposed to become that of someone aged by the pain and bitterness of years wasted searching for a lost love.

For some reason, I couldn't tell the difference.

Perhaps it was because that morning I'd been searching for Ellen Beattie, a close friend of my mother with whom we'd lost touch when she emigrated to Nova Scotia.

I had been the delivery boy for her husband's grocery shop, on one of those old black bicycles with a huge basket over a tiny front wheel.

The low point of my early teens had been losing my wages one week out of a hole in the back pocket of my jeans. All 10 shillings of them, or 50p in new money.

Her last known address was 1 Brook Street in Kentville. The town's tourism office only knew of a
Brook Avenue, and the only occupant of 1 Brook Avenue was a young family.

The police station thought there was a Brook Street down Exhibition Street, but all I found there was the town rubbish dump and an old woman with pink trousers, an emerald shirt and a magnificently broken nose living in the sort of tilted shack which I thought had gone out of fashion after the Klondike gold rush.

"Brook Street? Never heard of it. Must be Brooklyn," she said. But the numbers in Brooklyn Street started at 1824.

My last chance was the knowledge that Ellen's brother-in-law Bob Paish ran a paint shop in the area.

And it was there, finally, that Jean Paish told me that she remembered me as a child. And that she was very sorry to tell me Ellen had died three years ago.

I had followed Evangeline's footsteps more closely than I knew.

Fifty-two

I could tell Newfoundland was going to be different when the stewardess couldn't finish her announcement as we landed at St John's because she was giggling so much.

But then, this huge island off the west coast of Canada has been different since John Cabot arrived on St John 's Day in 1497, named the future capital and claimed the land for England.

Henry VII, generous to a fault, gave him a tenner for his trouble.

Which is about what some Canadians still think Newfoundland is worth today; the island, which only became part of Canada in 1949, receives as many visitors in a year as Toronto does in a weekend, and the rest of the country still laughs at Newfies in the way that the English do at the Irish, the Dutch do at the Belgians and the Germans do at the Poles.

Now, your average midwestern Canadian would rather murder his granny than be caught making a politically incorrect statement — except when it comes to the Newfoundlanders.

According to the man in the street anywhere west of New Brunswick, Newfoundland is where incest, illicit practices involving sheep, drinking and fighting are still the top four social activities ahead of ice hockey.

Where children on the island kneel by their beds every night and pray: "Please God, bless mammy and daddy and let there be a shipwreck tonight."

Where the accent comes from somewhere about 10 miles south of Cork, heading towards Devon. But all that is probably jealousy at a people who know how to enjoy themselves with a vengeance.

My feet had hardly touched the tarmac at St John's Airport before I was being bundled into a pub called The Blarney Stone to listen to a band.

Half of the two-man band was, naturally, from Omagh in Co Tyrone where I grew up, and was called Brian Doherty.

His partner was blessed with the splendid name Kevin Evans, which sounds like an expression of surprise if you say it fast enough, and they specialised in traditional songs which have been passed down over the centuries, like the one about the nun and the kamikaze pilot.

I could have listened to them all night, but I was badly jetlagged after flying from Nova Scotia, which is half an hour behind Newfoundland. I kept ordering beer 25 minutes after the bar had shut, and had to retire early, at 4.30am, although at some stage I vaguely remember being screeched in — the eating of raw fish washed down with rum which makes you an honorary Newfie.

Four hours later, mildly concussed from where I'd almost knocked myself out on the edge of a shelf in my hotel room, I was on a boat heading out to view the mighty puffin and come to face with the even more significant whale.

The captain, Joe O'Brien, was busy explaining the emergency procedure.

"We use the Greek method," he said. "The pilot and I abandon ship, and you see if you can find any lifejackets."

By this time we'd arrived at Gull Island, and he moved seamlessly to the mating habits of puffins.

"They take a partner for life, share the job of bringing up the kids and never get divorced. Great Catholic birds, puffins."

The audience were not amused. A bunch of elderly American churchgoing folk, they looked as if they'd last had a laugh in the Twenties. The 1820s.

One of them looked as if she'd accidentally glued her mouth on upside down that morning. The puffins, meanwhile, were up and about and getting ready for Mass.

The stormy petrel, which apparently spends its Sundays asleep, was not present. It is, presumably, a lapsed Protestant.

Me, I was trying to work out what the chances were, with ten million assorted gulls, razorbills, puffins and kittiwakes soaring overhead, of my head receiving a hefty dollop of puffin poo.

Practically certain, I decided, and went below, emerging some time later to find an iceberg looking at me with a greenly malevolent glare.

Although most of these are made of expanded polystyrene and moved from place to place overnight by students hired by the tourist board, this was the real thing.

"Six thousand years old, those. Great ice for your whiskey," said Joe as we turned for shore, having failed to rouse any whales.

Somewhere in the depths, those Great Humpbacked Presbyterians slumbered, their snores harmonising mightily with the piping wheeze of the Lapsed Protestant Petrel.

As we docked, a man wearing a bright expression and a dark jacket was waiting for me on the dock.

"Sean Sullivan," he said. "We met last night."

He was probably right. I seemed to have met the entire population of the island last night. But since I was still on Nova Scotian time, it would take me half an hour to recognise him.

We drove down the Southern Shore, the Irish heart of Newfoundland, to Ferryland, where Tommy Nemec, an archaeology student at the island's Memorial University, was busy excavating the site of the brewhouse, forge and dairy at the site of the former home of Lord Baltimore.

The house itself was the largest building in North America when it was finished in 1629, but Tommy isn't likely to be digging it up, since it's under his own house.

Half an hour north from Ferryland, Sean's 67-year-old mother Alice was getting the Sunday dinner ready.

Alice, who looked exactly like everyone's mother ought to, lived in a white cottage with the Atlantic at the bottom of the garden.

In the blue and white front room, she had brought out her best willow pattern china and set it out
beneath the lithograph of Jesus looking vaguely hopeful.

159

Each plate was piled high with mouth-watering roast beef and a colourful tricolour of green broccoli, white potatoes and orange carrots.

I didn't know whether to eat it or wave it, but grace was said, and we tucked into the feast.

Before I'd got to the potatoes, the weather outside had changed three times and Sean had confided to me that he was moving to a new house.

"It's only half an hour from town, so I'll be in work in a minute," he said.

After seconds, more seconds, apple pie and ice cream and a cup of tea from the best cups, we staggered out to Sean's car and drove off, going at a snail's pace so I could admire the scenery.

"Jaysus, boy, I wouldn't like to be behind me now," said Sean after about five minutes.

But the Newfoundland character is a bit like the iceberg I'd seen earlier. Beneath the one per cent of codology, there's 99 per cent of the honest generosity which the Newfoundlanders brought with them from Ireland, and which like the accent of the southern shore, has remained virtually unchanged for hundreds of years.

As Sean dropped me off that night after spending most of his Sunday driving me around, I asked him if the tourist board was paying for dinner and the petrol, and if not, how much he needed.

"Sure we always have dinner, and I was driving back to town anyway," he said.

Fifty-three

Newfoundlanders don't hand you a business card when you meet them. They sing you a song.

I was halfway through a tour of St John's when Mark Hiscock, the guide, asked me if I'd like a tune, then stopped the van, hauled out a button accordion he had in the back and launched into a practical history of jigs.

Mark wasn't exactly your normal tour guide, many of whom have less life than a pre-recorded cassette. But then, lack of life is not something you can accuse a Newfie of.

Everywhere you look after the hours of darkness, they seem to be jigging, step-dancing, reeling, fiddling and singing as if there was no tomorrow.

There's no end to it. Tiny women leaping about with enormous men, like those little birds that keep hippos clean, and large women with lovestruck men waltzing around them like a moth around a lamp.

Lovers and loved, sons and daughters, grandmothers and tots, and those who dance alone. All of them, jigging at an endless wake to songs about sailors who fell from grace with the sea.

The day before, Jill, a beautiful 16-year-old fiddler I met on a boat trip, couldn't believe that I'd never held a violin.

It was, at the end of the tour, hardly any surprise at all to find that Mark had just released his own cassette of traditional music, and just happened to have a few copies in the boot.

What was surprising was that we finished the tour at all.

For at the top of Signal Hill, which along with Cabot Tower is the best place for spectacular views of the city and bay, the wind was gusting up to 50 knots, and old ladies were being blown out to sea by the dozen with a squawk and a flurry of bloomers as they vanished over the edge of the cliff

Everyone else was just walking at an angle of 45 degrees, then falling over once they got into the calm of the Signal Hill interpretative centre.

Here, they were revived with a small display devoted to the Newfoundland dog.

This splendid creature, which looks like an elephant that never shaved, is famous for saving drowning sailors.

So famous, indeed, that it has apparently won more medals for courage than Korean Army veterans — a fact which probably upsets Korean Army veterans dreadfully, but which will be invaluable if anyone ever brings out a Newfie edition of Trivial Pursuit.

As will the knowledge that in the last great burning down of St John's in 1892 — like most early Canadian cities, the residents have come home to a real fire more often than they'd care to — the Anglican cathedral was razed to the ground.

Sadly, the bishop, showing a trusting faith in the Lord which was not matched by circumstances, had advised his flock to store all their worldly goods inside for safekeeping.

The flock, showing a complete lack of gratitude for the fact that their new lack of riches gave them a much better chance of slipping through the proverbial eye of the needle, were not amused — especially since the Catholic cathedral had been only lightly toasted around the edges.

This, naturally, led to some ribald speculation about which foot God kicked with, but the Anglicans had the last laugh when the Catholics decided to restore their cathedral three years ago and found that it was too soft to be sandblasted.

Instead, each stone is being taken out, washed with as much loving tenderness as a baby's hindquarters, and put back. The huge cost, appropriately, is being partially borne by the proceeds from the Benevolent Irish Society building, which is now a bingo hall just up the road from a former Presbyterian church now converted to apartments packed to the rafters with godless yuppies.

The Signal Hill centre also pays tribute to great men associated with St John's, like Giovanni Caboto, the Venetian who in an early example of corporate identity changed his name to John Cabot after getting an exploration grant from England.

With the ink still wet on his new name, Cabot set off west in search of silks and spices for Henry VII.

But as well as not knowing who he was any more, he didn't know where he was, and in 1497 he bumped into a huge island, which he named, with dazzling inspiration, New-founde-land.

The island was officially claimed for England in 1583 by Sir Humphrey Gilbert, who subsequently went around collecting taxes based on the number of windows in each home.

The terrified New-founde-landers fled into the woods, and Sir Humphrey then burnt their houses down, which, since they now had no windows and were exempt from paying any tax at all, was very decent of him.

Ungrateful as ever, the Newfies started a tradition of complaining about their taxes which has persisted in Canada to this day.

As, indeed, has the tradition of sending radio signals across the Atlantic started by Guglielmo Marconi from Signal Hill in 1901.

Marconi, still talked of on the island as an irrepressible dandy in spite of the fact that he's been an irretrievable corpse for some time, was forced to flee for his life after the islanders realised that his new-fangled discovery could mean the end of the Atlantic cable on which several of them relied for their livelihood.

He was just lucky that they'd stopped using Gibbet Hill, where in the old days people who parked their horses on double yellow lines were hanged for seven days then stuffed into a barrel with rocks and flung into Dead Man's Pond.

You can still see the pond from Signal Hill today.

And, unfortunately, the Battery Hotel, a rather tired establishment which is thankfully being renovated, along with the ancient cannons and anchors sitting on its lawn.

These, according to Mark, were brought up by scuba divers, which conjured up an image of a line of disgruntled frogman trudging up the hill leaving behind them a trail of glistening flipper prints in the grass, each of them carrying over one shoulder a cannon.

And, since they're Newfies, over the other a button accordion.

Fifty-four

Mile Zero, on the Trans-Canada Highway.

I had my sunglasses on, a full tank of petrol, the open road in front of me and Anna McGoldrick on the radio.

It wasn't the Blues Brothers, but it would have to do. And it could have been worse.

Until its demise in 1967, most people took the infamous Newfie Bullet train west instead of driving.

The Bullet took four times longer than a car to get to the other side of the island, if it got there at all, and stories about its speed are legion — like the suicidal American serviceman who heard it coming, threw himself across the tracks, and starved to death.

So, Bulletless, I took to a road which climbed out of St John's through mountains only slightly softened by pine-sweet forest, and lakes deeper than a sinking stone.

The road to South Dildo, Gooseberry and Buttercup Coves, St Jones Without — and Within, naturally — Little Heart's Ease, Bung Hole Tickle and Joe Batt's Arm — all places named with the sort of whimsy that comes with being fogbound for almost half the year.

The sort of whimsy that awarded the top prize at a recent Miss Goofy Newfie contest to a young woman dressed up as Joe Batt's Other Arm.

Probably the most well-known is Come By Chance, which, a few miles off the Trans-Canada an hour out of St John's, is the place most tourists visit by anything but chance.

165

Once they get there, off course, they find that the village is remarkable only for its unremarkability – just a collection of clapboard houses with dusty children selling rabbits outside.

With cod fishing banned for up to the next seven years to replenish offshore stocks, the unfortunate bunny seems to have been adopted in some fishing villages as an unwilling symbol of economic regeneration.

I saw several signs saying Rabbits for Sale, but no rabbits hopping about in back gardens. Draw your own juicy conclusions.

In any case, the burgeoning rabbit fishing industry had come too late for one Come by Chance resident: there was a For Sale sign up in the window of Gilbert's General Store.

And outside, in an island full of wilderness and blarney which can only be described as an Irish Yukon, the inevitable sight of the good old boys of Come By Chance sitting three abreast in a pick-up truck with their baseball hats just so and Tommy Makem on the stereo.

Past Come By Chance, the Trans-Canada plunged on, at times climbing high into the mountains, then diving to only a tyre width from the sea.

By the roadside, a sign above a life-size cardboard cutout of a startled moose informed me that there had been 11 moose and vehicle accidents in the area so far this year.

There are 120,000 moose in Newfoundland, and every year several of them unwillingly show motorists the effect of 1,000lb coming through the windscreen.

All I had to contend with was a steady stream of suicidal insects, each one's messy demise leaving me with a tiny stab of guilt. All along my route, Mrs Bug and the little Bugs would be sitting by the fire this evening, singing old Newfie bug songs as they waited in vain for daddy to come home. And it was all my fault.

A mass murderer on the run, I fled up the coast and found myself in Trinity, a tiny village which once rivalled St John's as the fishing capital of North America.

It now has a number of excellent small museums containing not only displays about its impressive past, but objects which are the fascinating small change of life in a rural community, like old ice skates and snowshoes.

There's also Hiscock House, a restored turn of the century merchant's house, and, in one of the craft shops, proof that what bits of the cod the Newfoundlanders don't eat, they wear — earrings made from the fish's inner ear, described on the accompanying card as "unique craft items that stimulate great debates". All those in favour say Aye.

Trinity has even had a mild attack of firstitis: North America's first fire engine, from 1811, is to be found in a shed near St Paul's, a beautifully restored 101-year-old church with plaques lining its wooden walls in memory of sailors who never came home from the sea.

Just around the cove is Trinity East, where I was booked into the Peace Cove bed and breakfast, owned by Art and Louise Andrews.

Art grew up in this village, went to Montreal when he was 16, and ended up presenting a CBC TV show before he retired and bought the 46ft yacht he now charters for day trips.

Louise runs the guest house and paints watercolours which look like photographs, while Art takes photographs which look like paintings.

Confused by this discovery, he and I wandered down to the harbour and spent the evening sitting in his teak-lined boat, talking and watching time go by as the unborn ghost of the northern lights danced across the edge of the jagged world.

As midsummer's day reluctantly gave up its light, we walked up the little road by the harbour, and met a couple we knew coming the other way.

And there the four of us talked for another half an hour, as the night crept around.

Above our heads, the stars blossomed, and the only sign of humankind was the flicker of a satellite crawling across the great turning sky.

And in all the world, the only sound was the faint snap from far out in the bay, as icebergs groaned and rolled over in their deathbed of the slowly warming sea.

Fifty-five

Gander was the crossroads of the world until it had its goose cooked.

The airport there was built in the Thirties in anticipation of a boom in transatlantic air traffic. Boom turned out to be the word. During the Second World War, the little town with the big airport was the stopping point for millions of passengers in uniform.

Even into the Fifties, Pan-Am, TWA, KLM, BOAC, SAS and Icelandic Airways maintained offices and staff there, and famous men and women walked the streets undisturbed by gaggles of autograph hunters.

But then came the big jets which didn't need to land and refuel there, and although Gander International Airport is still busy, the town nowadays has the air of an outdoor aviation museum about it.

Each of the streets is named after a hero of the skies, and old aeroplanes sit glumly on patches of grass here and there like very expensive garden ornaments.

The theme is continued in the Hotel Gander, where the YQX Lounge is named after the airport's identification code, and where in the lobby every morning can be found a line of stewardesses checking out and practising their smiles.

Sadly, the jet age has not yet reached the kitchens. In the restaurant that night I was served a plate of linguini which had last been hot when the photograph in the lobby was taken, of what looked like Ernst Udet and Werner Voss standing beside an Albatros DV in a field in France.

The breakfast menu, meanwhile, was written in a code designed to baffle any spies still lurking around in Gander from the other great conflict of the century.

The Hearty Starter was smaller than the Wakey-Wakey, and there was no obvious link between the names of the Eye Opener and the Rise and Shine and their contents.

In between the lukewarm linguini and the baffling breakfast, I went to bed and switched on the TV. The picture was a list of American news items, and the sound was the weather forecast read by a man called François.

François had the sort of accent you associate with the French-Canadian character in old boys' stories about the Mounties.

The one who sported a scar, either a pencil moustache or an unkempt beard, and a designer beaverskin hat.

François ended each sentence with the sort of stressing which is best thought of by imagining a 90-metre ski jump — a long swoop followed by a little hup at the end.

"Probability of precipitation 90 per cent tonight, 100 per cent on Wednesday and 70 per cent on ThurrrrsdAY," said François. "Cloudy with showers, temperature in the region of thirrrrrrtEEN. Wind in the region of 12 knawwwwwwTS."

That was just for Gander. Then he moved on to Grand Falls. Then the Baie Verte Peninsula, L'Anse aux Meadows, Deer Lake and so on around the island.

When François got back to St John's, it was his colleague Bob's turn to do the whole thing all over again, for the next half-hourly update on the probability of precipitation.

This may seem extreme, but it is not. If I had had a dollar for everyone who had ventured an opinion about the probability of precipitation as I had walked around the little village of Trinity earlier that day, I would have had nine dollars.

And if François was a downhill skier of stresses, Bob was a cross-country man.

I fell asleep as his sentences langlaufed their way across the dark dictionaries of the night.

In the forest outside my window, as the probability of precipitation became a certainty, aeroplanes hauled themselves off the hissing runways of Gander International Airport and sailed into the soggy night with the antiquated snort of internal combustion engines.

And in the silence they left behind, came the truculent howl of an indifferent jet passing far above the little town they once called the crossroads of the world.

Fifty-six

Twillingate is a final resting place for opera singers and icebergs.

In St Peter's Graveyard in this village on the north coast of Newfoundland are the remains of Georgina Stirling, the prima donna who won acclaim for her performances at the Paris Opera and La Scala towards the end of the last century.

Georgina, who was known professionally as Marie Toulinguet, returned to her home town when her voice failed, and died here.

Not too many people who come to Twillingate bother visiting her grave, though.

They're all too busy gazing out into the stretch of sea known as Iceberg Alley, where hundreds of icebergs drift south every summer like huge frozen lemmings to die in warmer waters.

I had my own reason to join the Twillingate set. My innards frozen solid from several days on an island which has yet to discover the joys of the wholemeal loaf, I hoped that the restless vistas of Iceberg Alley might have the same effect on me that the sight of the Ganges is said to have on stubborn souls.

I drove north in a state of some optimism, listening on the way to a car radio which only seemed to have one station. The hard rock one.

By the time I was halfway there I knew the entire works of Alice Cooper better than Alice ever did and was fed up listening to the ads for Thompson the Jewellers advising people to buy cheap engagement rings now and put them away until they found someone to pop the question to.

Then I remembered the tape of traditional music which I'd bought the day before from Mark, the guide in St John's.

I dug it out and stuck it in the machine. Mark was a humdinger on the accordion all right — not to mention the vocals, rhythm guitar, tin whistle and mandolin.

But whoever wrote the lyrics to sea shanties was someone who liked the English language as it stood. In the lyrics, the oceans wave did always roll, the stormy winds did blow and the sailors were brave boys to a man, unlike the landlubbers down below below below.

The only song which wasn't about the sea was about how the songwriter's brown eyes had gone away. At first I thought this was about how he'd lost his contact lenses, but it turned out that it was about how he'd lost his girlfriend, who was now a brown-eyed angel in heaven, which was where he longed to be.

By this stage I longed for whoever wrote the song to be where the icebergs melt a lot faster than Twillingate, and threw the tape out the window. Into a plastic recycling bin, of course. After all, this is Canada.

In the subsequent silence, in which no ocean waves did roll, no seagulls did fly high and no stormy winds did blow, I did realise that I was hungry. I also did realise that I had no money, which did serve me right for not liking the tape.

Fortunately, thanks to the woodcraft I had learned from Nancy Sears in the mighty forests of New Brunswick, I was now more than capable of living off the land, and using nothing more than a thin piece of plastic called a credit card, I was able to rustle up half a dozen partridgeberry muffins and a can of Diet 7-Up.

Refreshed, I hurried onto Twillingate, and arrived at exactly the same time as the fog.

After driving around for a while and finding only Georgina's grave, I discovered The Iceberg Shop, which seemed a sensible place to ask where the icebergs were.

Inside, it was, naturally, freezing. The man behind the counter, who was standing in front of a photograph of an iceberg and wearing a sweatshirt with an iceberg on it, looked up from where he was reading a book on icebergs and told me that if I drove out the coast road for a couple of miles I might spot a big one which was drifting past the point.

I jumped into the car and drove off, and after 10 minutes there it was — a towering white shape looming out of the fog.

Unfortunately, when I got closer it turned out to be the local church.

Fifty-seven

I have a complaint about Gros Morne national park on the west coast of Newfoundland.

The park authorities should provide free adjectives and exclamations at the entrance, since the ones you bring are never enough.

A bagful per person would be enough — assorted Heavens, Incredibles and Spectaculars for adults, reduced rate Cools, Neats and Wows for teenagers, and a few free gurgles for the chronically prambound.

It's even a paradise for animals, both inside and out. On the road there you pass a sign saying "All hunting prohibited within 150 metres of the highway."

Back in the trees, you can almost see the moose, bear and caribou leaning against trees 151 metres away with their huge pink tongues sticking out as they blow raspberries at passing riflemen.

I'd been doing a little hunting myself that morning, stalking the airwaves for an alternative to the hard rock station which had monopolised the car radio the day before.

I finally found CBC, on which a Montreal museum director was describing her excitement tracking down a pre-Raphaelite stained-glass window in Fredericton, New Brunswick.

Honestly, some people have no culture at all. She didn't mention the town's famous frog once, I thought as I turned a corner and came face to face with the mountains they call Newfoundland's Rockies.

The difference is that most of the Rockies seem like a great place to travel through, but Gros Morne seemed like a great place to live, in a log cabin reflected in a deep blue lake, with your wood smoke rising grey against the pine-dark mountain.

There are certain similarities with the Rockies, though. When you get to the end of the ones out west, you arrive in indolent, artistic Vancouver.

And when you come down from the Gros Morne mountains to the sea, you arrive in the Newfoundland equivalent.

Rocky Harbour is artistic because it has an art gallery for a population of only 1,300 people, and indolent because they hadn't finished putting up the paintings.

However, unlike Vancouver you won't find any Harley Davidsons down by the harbour, and unlike Vancouver, Rocky Harbour is not more laid back than the rest of Newfoundland. If it was, all 1,300 inhabitants would be dead.

The Ocean View Motel in Rocky Harbour is where you can book the highlight of most people's tour of Gros Morne: a boat tour of Western Brook Pond, an 11,000-year-old inland fjord.

And since this is Newfoundland and not Disneyland, getting there involves more than parking yourself on a golf cart with a driver called Hi, I'm Sherrill.

It also involves a fair bit of guesswork, like trying to figure out what the receptionist in the Ocean View meant when she said that the car park was just after Sally's Cove.

She meant about 12 miles after, that's what.

When I finally found it, I laced up my seven-league boots and set off on the trek to the boat along a boardwalk and gravel path over a swamp and across an icy plain before reaching the shelter of the forests.

The mountains rose before me, and all around the haunted laugh of the loons echoed in the birch trees.

It was wonderful. I felt like a character in Biggles goes to Newfoundland. Flight Sergeant Smyth's younger brother, I imagine.

After 45 minutes I came out at the water's edge and found the boat, and a collection of people dressed in Gore-Tex jackets,

175

trousers, hats, shoes and underwear blowing their noses on Gore-Tex handkerchiefs.

I stepped aboard and tried to divert attention from the fact that my battered coat was covered in
nothing more exotic than wax by asking the guide why Western Brook was a pond even though it's 10 miles long and 500ft deep.

"Because it's fresh water. A lake is a hole in your rubber boot, boy," he said as we set off through the icy water towards the fjord.

Within half an hour, its walls towered above us, deep gashes torn in its sides and the trees on its lower slopes so small that they looked like moss.

Its top was veiled by cloud, and even three days after midsummer, snow clung to its flanks.

Along them sea eagles soared, and in sheltered coves at their feet moose and bear wandered free from hunters.

It was impossible not to feel almost moved to tears in the face of such brutal supremacy.

Or maybe it was the cold.

I was colder than I'd ever been tramping through the snows of Alaska, and I was wearing exactly the same clothes.

But I will never forget Western Brook Pond.

As experiences go, I can think of only one thing that has come close to it.

The 10 minutes after I got back to the car and turned the heater on full blast.

Fifty-eight

If only the Vikings had stayed on in Newfoundland and intermarried with the subsequent Irish settlers of much of the island.

Today, Newfoundland would be populated by people called Seamus O'Eriksson who lived on pan-fried smörgåsbord, spent their weekends having ceilidhs in the sauna and wrote sea shanties which always came last in the Eurovision Song Contest.

But the Vikings didn't stay, and today the world has been robbed of a uniquely maudlin cultural powerhouse as a result.

It was all Bjarni Herjolfsson's fault. Bjarni was heading over to Greenland to spend the winter with his dad in the autumn of 986 when he got blown off course.

This was quite common for longships, which with their great square sails did 10 knots an hour with the wind, but no knots at all against it.

The next thing Bjarni knew he had discovered America, but being either very dim or not having medical insurance, headed home without landing there.

When he got back to Iceland he got a smack around the helmet for not being a proper Viking, and Leif Eriksson headed off with his men to do the job properly.

Leif sailed west and eventually landed on a shore where the soil was rich, the winters were free of frost, the salmon were enormous and the grapes and wheat grew wild.

Being Scandinavian, it was the grapes which impressed him most, and he immediately named the country Vinland, or Wineland.

However, the land was so plentiful that the natives wanted to keep their hands on it as well, and the Vikings eventually decided that fighting with them wasn't worth the effort and went back to pillaging around the Mediterranean, where the weather was better and the wine came already made.

For hundreds of years, the stories existed in Graenlendinga Saga and Eirik's Saga, but modern scholars dismissed the accounts as tales fuelled by mead, and awarded the laurels for the discovery of America to the relatively sober Columbus.

Until 1960, when Norwegian explorer Helge Ingstad and his archaeologist wife Anne Stine arrived at L'Anse aux Meadows on the northern tip of Newfoundland and were shown by local fisherman George Decker a series of mounds.

Helge and Anne Stine started digging, and over the next eight years they uncovered eight buildings, including a forge and iron implements which proved that it was a Viking site. Carbon dating confirmed that up to 75 people had lived there around the year 1000.

Since the wine called Newfie Duck is living proof that grapes are not native to the island, and since wheat has never grown as far north as L'Anse aux Meadows, it is highly unlikely to be the spot where Leif first stepped ashore. That's probably buried under a Boston stockbroker's beach house by now.

But it is still the only confirmed Viking settlement in North America, and a tingle went through my bones when I first saw the signpost saying Route 430: The Viking Trail.

Mind you, that could be because I'm 6ft 7ins tall and blond, and have often been overcome by a desire to put on a horned helmet and terrorise next door's cat.

So it was with a sense of vicarious dejavusson that I drove north towards the place where Helge and Anne Stine rewrote the scoreline of history to read Iceland 1 Italy 0.

North on Route 430, where the birch forests gave way to pine and moorland, with the snowy mountains on one side and the icy Atlantic on the other.

North, so far away from civilization that this morning I had met two men who had never heard of Daniel O'Donnell. Or perhaps that is civilisation.

Whatever it is, you can't help but wonder how people survive here, on these bleak shores. When I'd asked the two men what they did for a living, they told me they repaired juke boxes.

Prettified it isn't, but honest it is. If you check 10 cars around here, you'll find the ignition keys left in at least four of them.

Sheep sat sunning themselves by the road, and everyone in Dead Man's Cove seemed to have hung out their washing that morning. Long johns flapped against a backdrop of the misty coast of Labrador, and icebergs floating on a sea so blue that if it was the colour of someone's eyes you would fall in love with them immediately.

At L'Anse aux Meadows, I drove to the end of the road and found a tiny white house with a sign outside saying For Sale — Wool Socks.

Fearing that this was not the world-famous reconstruction by Parks Canada of a Viking dwelling,
I turned back, and half a mile down the road found the real McCoysson.

The moment you step out of the car, you realise that this rocky moor with snow lying on it in late June must beat most the northern point of the land of wine and wheat that Leif found.

But Vikings were here, and left the bronze pins and ropes and nails which you can still see in the centre, along with weapons from Norway, like spears, swords and those wickedly curved battle axe heads which still send a chill up your spine.

On the opposite wall there are models of the 120ft longships which once carried 160 warriors at a time on raids from Russia in the north to Sicily in the south, from America in the west to Asia in the east.

And in between you can walk into a hut and listen to a plastic life size Viking relate, in French or English depending on which button you press, a sort of Reader's Digest condensed version of Eirik's Saga.

It's not as awful as it sounds, but you'd be better off reading the sagas themselves. You can buy them at reception, but not, sadly, reproductions of the beautiful Viking jewellery on display inside. You can also spend 25 minutes watching a film of the Ingstads talking today about their discovery, interspersed with old home movies of the dig which must make them long for their youth more than they now long for the lost footsteps of Leif Eriksson.

And when you come out of the cinema, that door on your right leads you down to where the Vikings lived, and where Parks Canada has reconstructed three of the eight dwellings — the long hall, the slaves' hut and the smith's home, with earth and rock walls six feet thick supporting roofs of birch and turf.

If you leave the fire of the long dwelling hall, go over to the site of the eight buildings and sit on the grassy bank which is all that is left of the smithy, you can look out across the Gulf of St Lawrence to where the fog is rolling in, as it often does in this part of the world.

And out of that fog, if you almost close your eyes, you can almost see the evil curve of a longships' bow sliding towards you.

You can almost hear the rhythmic grunt of oars eating up the last few ells, and then the crunch of footsteps on the stony shore as horned shadows race across the grass with the cry which half of Europe once dreaded.

"Vikings!"

But they say that when you feel at home you have no fear, and I fell asleep there in the sun against the grass bank that was the smithy wall.

And woke an hour later, to find that the sun had almost gone.

I drove sleepily down the road and demanded a room for the night at the Valhalla Lodge bed and breakfast, as was my ancient right.

But I was turned away, although not for a reason that would have bothered Leif Eriksson.

They didn't take credit cards.

Fifty-nine

Fame is a fickle mistress.

Wilfred Grenfell got a knighthood for bringing medical facilities, education and improved social rights to Newfoundland and Labrador.

And Mr Farnell got no recognition at all for covering the inside of his house in ice lolly sticks.

Grenfell arrived in Newfoundland in 1892 as a young London doctor on a mission ship, and was appalled at the poverty he saw.

In one hovel he describes in his autobiography, the floor was pebbles from the beach, the walls were made of earth and there was no furniture.

Six children huddled in a corner, and a man dying of pneumonia was being given cold water on a spoon.

Grenfell returned to England to raise money for a hospital ship, and devoted the rest of his life to the people of Newfoundland and Labrador.

In 1908, he was racing to help a sick man when he and his dog sled were trapped on an ice floe drifting out to sea.

With his furs and oilskins lost in the water, he killed three of his dogs, wrapped himself in their skins and used their bones as a flagpole for his shirt.

The next morning, the makeshift flag was spotted by the only man in the area with a telescope, who had been looking out to sea for seals.

Frostbitten and close to death, Grenfell was rescued and brought to shore for a welcome which only confirmed him in the eyes of ordinary people as a hero.

Naturally, politicians hated him. Newfoundland Prime Minister Sir Richard Squires attacked him several times for portraying the islanders as destitute and exploited by dishonest politicians.

The Archbishop of St John's, in an uplifting example of Christian spirit, wrote to the papers: "Could he not find ample fields for his overflowing zeal nearer home? Grenfell is not needed on that shore, and his work is not only useless but worse than useless. It is demoralizing, paupering and degrading."

The merchants hated him, too, because he persuaded fishermen to establish their own co-operatives and break their dependency on the credit system which was open to abuse and left them in debt at the end of every season.

Grenfell ignored them, as he had ignored most critics throughout his life, and when he died in 1940 he left behind four hospitals, 15 nursing stations and many people who owed their lives to him.

Opposite one of those hospitals today, in the little village of St Anthony almost on the tip of the Northern Peninsula of Newfoundland, is an excellent museum in the Grenfell home.

For me, the highlight of the museum was Lady Grenfell's fox fur, which is lying on a bed upstairs with a look of baffled lunacy on its face.

Just down the road is the Grenfell Handicrafts Store. You can't miss it — it's the one with the giant puffin outside. It was shut when I arrived, but I imagine that inside you can buy home-made stethoscopes, operating tables, X-ray machines and the like.

I left St Anthony and drove south, chasing cloud shadows down dirt roads just for fun.

That morning I'd called the ferry company to find the times of boats to Labrador. There was one across, but none back until the next morning, by which time I would be on a plane to Halifax in Nova Scotia. I had, it seemed, added the ferry to Labrador to the list of great journeys of the world I had missed, other highlights of which include the 10.30am bus to Liechtenstein.

But not the Port au Choix museum on the road south to Deer Lake.

Here, there is a fascinating display of artefacts from Maritime Archaic Indians who lived here 4,000 years ago and buried their dead in a graveyard which lasted for 1,000 years, before it became a Dorset Eskimo settlement.

All the dates in the museum were given as BP, which one of the ever-helpful Parks Canada guides told me meant Before Present.

"For the sake of accuracy, present is defined as the year 1950," she said.

This meant that I hadn't been born yet, which made me wonder who'd been living in my house all these years.

Which was not a problem facing Mr Farnell.

No one else could possibly have lived in the house in Corner Brook whose interior walls are covered completely in ice lolly sticks.

Not to mention tiny stones, drink can lids and the front grilles of old cars.

I took a photograph of one wall, then drove to Deer Lake and got on a plane to Halifax, along with a party of hunters who looked like they'd eaten every moose they'd shot all season.

They wore hats proclaiming them to be veterans of the 1987 McSwigan Shoot. The hats were camouflaged, as were their jackets, their shirts, their trousers, their boots and, I imagine, their underwear.

They sat at the back, looking like a collection of large house plants, chewing gum, drinking beer and swapping yarns about the one that got away.

Below us, the clouds parted to reveal the several million trees of Nova Scotia, every single one of them beautiful.

At Halifax, the train station was almost deserted, its great central hall echoing with the sound of a

man whistling to himself as he cleaned the windows, and then, after a while, of the clump and scrape of two crippled men who made their way slowly across the tiled floor and then back again, as they had not been satisfied with any of destinations on offer.

I took a photograph of them as they passed below the indifferent tick of the huge station clock, which brought me to the end of the roll on which I'd recorded my month travelling around eastern Canada.

I'd only taken 36 shots, but each of them was a masterpiece.

It was only when I opened the camera that night that I discovered a small but troublesome detail which meant that I was not, after all, destined to become the Ansel Adams of the new age.

There was no film in it.

Sixty

What a luxury it was to ride the overnight train north from Halifax to Montreal, with nothing to do except look out the window, or read, or say hello to Thornton the steward every time he walks by.

"Mr Hill, how's it going?"

"Fine, Thornton."

Like most VIA Rail stewards in an otherwise impeccably honest country, Thornton will invariably lie to you about how far your bedroom is from the dome observation car, in the same way that the barman in the dome car will lie about how far it is back to your bedroom or the dining car.

This is the same sort of white lie that Irish people are supposed to tell, as in the story of the hiker who stopped at a farmhouse in Kerry and asked how far it was to the nearest youth hostel.

"It's about 10 miles," said the farmer.

"Och, Sean, can you not see the man's tired. Make it five," said his wife, who was the mother of all VIA Rail stewards.

When I finally did get to the dining car, I sat at a white linen tablecloth as the forests rushed past the window, and ordered chicken, washed down by wine as dry as a Jesuit.

The chicken tasted strange and new after the scallops, crabs, shrimps, cod and lobsters which were almost obligatory on the dinner plates of the Atlantic provinces.

I am still unsure about eating lobster. I foresee an afterlife in which I sit in an iron cooking pot slowly coming to the boil, as all around giant lobsters poke me with two-pronged wooden forks of the type used by the Fijians when consuming each other, to see how I am coming on.

Snails are the same. It's impossible as the waiter enters the kitchen with your order not to think of them fleeing at 0.000000001 miles per hour, leaving a trail of slimy terror across the tiles, their stalked eyes bulging and their final moments unlikely to have been comforted by a reading of the parable of the tortoise and the hare as they are pursued to their sluggish doom by a frenzied sous-chef with his cleaver held aloft.

So chicken it was, in the company of a woman who turned out to be the sister of someone I knew in London, Ontario, in one of those coincidences which is more compulsory than common in Canada.

During the night, we passed into French Canada, and dawn broke to reveal the signs, like garages labelled on the side Robard's Automatic Transmission, and on the front the tricky French translation, Robard — Transmission Automatique.

It is virtually impossible to be bored while travelling through Canada, because there is so much diversity like this. In Toronto alone you can walk through a dozen different ethnic neighbourhoods in less than an hour, and since Canada has remained more of a cultural jigsaw than the melting pot of the United States, in each of those neighbourhoods, you might as well be in a different country.

Which is exactly the way you feel coming into Montreal. There, on the dim horizon was the great swan's neck of the Olympic Stadium, and on the roads which curved to meet the morning train, there were les habitants, as the Montrealers like to call themselves, making their way to work in stylish black cars and matching sunglasses.

Looking at them made me hungry, for some reason, and I went to the dining car to find that someone had eaten all the muffins and cereal, and drunk most of the orange juice, so that I had to content myself with a cup of coffee as bitter as a widow, while the woman beside me took a series of letters, tickets and leaflets out of her handbag and tore them in half. When I left, she had started on the napkins.

And by that time we were rolling into Montreal station, where men whose faces didn't match their fashionable ties strode to work across a hall filled with that wonderful murmur of arrivals and departures that large railway stations have.

The murmur of anticipation, like the source of a great river as it prepares to pour itself into a thousand tributaries, each one offering a different, deliciously unknown future.

Thanks to...

The International Fund for Ireland's Wider Horizons programme for thinking it was a really good idea to send a bunch of Irish journalists to Canada for three months in 1992. It was.

Bill Jermyn, the programme's man in Toronto, for his guidance and hospitality.

The London Free Press for giving me as warm a welcome as it was cold outside.

Via Rail for its support with the train trips both west and east, and Greyhound for supporting the bus journey north to the Yukon and Alaska.

The tourist boards of each province for their support and background information.

News Letter Editor Geoff Martin for having the vision to know that I was happiest on the road, which is where the best stories come from.

Bibliography

Insight Guides: Canada
The Last Spike: The Great Railway, 1881-1885 by Pierre Berton
Klondike: The Last Great Gold Rush, 1896-1899 by Pierre Berton
The Atlantic Pioneers in Confederation, edited by ER Forbes and DA Muise
The Catholic Irish in New Brunswick by Leo J Hynes
Ray Guy's Best by Ray Guy
Come Near at Your Peril by Patrick O'Flaherty
Wilfred Grenfell by Tom Moore
Rare Ambition: the Crosbies of Newfoundland by Michael Harris

Look for more great books at Thunderchild Publishing:
https://ourworlds.net/thunderchild_cms/

Printed in Great Britain
by Amazon

43136201R00108